Up & Running
with WordPerfect
Library/Office PC

Up & Running with WordPerfect® Library/Office™ PC

Jeff Woodward

SYBEX®

San Francisco • Paris • Düsseldorf • Soest

Z
52
5
.W45
W049
1991

Acquisitions Editor: Dianne King
Series Editor: Joanne Cuthbertson
Editor: Tanya Kucak
Technical Editor: Maryann Brown
Word Processors: Paul Erickson, Lisa Mitchell
Book Designer: Elke Hermanowski
Icon Designer: Helen Bruno
Screen Graphics: Cuong Le
Desktop Production Artist: Charlotte Carter
Proofreader: Hilda van Genderen
Indexer: Nancy Guenther
Cover Designer: Archer Designs

SYBEX
Up & Running Books

The Up & Running series of books from SYBEX has been developed for committed, eager PC users who would like to become familiar with a wide variety of programs and operations as quickly as possible. We assume that you are comfortable with your PC and that you know the basic functions of word processing, spreadsheets, and database management. With this background, Up & Running books will show you in 20 steps what particular products can do, and how to use them.

Up & Running books are designed to save you time and money. First, you can avoid purchase mistakes by previewing products before you buy them—exploring their features, strengths, and limitations. Second, once you decide to purchase a product, you can learn its basics quickly by following the 20 steps—even if you are a beginner.

What this book provides

The first step always covers software installation in relation to hardware requirements. You'll learn whether the program can operate with your available hardware as well as various methods for starting the program. The second step introduces the program's user interface. The remaining 18 steps demonstrate the program's essential functions, using examples and short descriptions.

Contents & structure

A clock shows the amount of time you can expect to spend at your computer for each step. Naturally, you'll need much less time if you only read through the step rather than complete it at your computer.

Special symbols & notes

You can also focus on particular points by scanning the short notes in the margins and locating the sections you are most interested in.

In addition, three symbols highlight particular sections of text:

 The Action symbol highlights important steps that you will carry out.

 The Tip symbol indicates a practical hint or special technique.

 The Warning symbol alerts you to a potential problem and suggestions for avoiding it.

We have structured the Up & Running books so that the busy user spends little time studying documentation and is not burdened with unnecessary text. An Up & Running book cannot, of course, replace a lengthier book that contains advanced applications. However, you will get the information you need to put the program to practical use and to learn its basic functions in the shortest possible time.

We welcome your comments

SYBEX is very interested in your reactions to the Up & Running series. Your opinions and suggestions will help all of our readers, including yourself. Please send your comments to: SYBEX Editorial Department, 2021 Challenger Drive, Alameda, CA 94501.

Preface:
Up & Running with WordPerfect Library/Office PC

If you are like most computer users, you are always looking for the best way to manage and manipulate data and to organize your professional and personal tasks. Consequently, you continually look for those computer programs that will enable you to achieve the most effective working environment. Office PC version 3.0, which replaces WordPerfect Library version 2.0, provides several programs designed to facilitate the computer tasks you perform on a daily basis. These programs include the Office PC Shell, Calculator, Calendar, File Manager, Notebook, and Macro/Program Editor. In this book I will discuss all of these programs except the Macro/Program Editor, which is an advanced program beyond the scope of this entry-level book.

Office PC is a desktop organizer

The Office PC Shell allows you to start your favorite WordPerfect and non-WordPerfect Corporation programs with a single keystroke, run two or more programs at the same time, switch quickly between active programs, and move text from one program to another. **Steps 2–6** cover the Shell.

Office PC Shell

The Calculator program includes five types of calculators: Arithmetic, Financial, Scientific, Statistical, and Programmer. These calculators, covered in **Steps 7–10**, can assist you in performing a great many of your mathematical tasks.

Calculator

The Calendar is the perfect place to organize your daily memos, appointments, and to-do tasks, as well as keep track of the date. The Calendar has an alarm system that alerts you to an impending appointment from within any program that you may be working in, as long as you start that program from the Shell. **Steps 11–14** discuss the Calendar.

Calendar

File Manager

If you don't understand DOS very well, you can use File Manager to create directories, and to locate, delete, copy, and rename files, plus much more. You can accomplish all these DOS tasks without ever having to type a DOS command. **Steps 15–16** cover the File Manager.

Notebook

You can use the Notebook to maintain a record of phone numbers, addresses, birthdays, and other information for your friends, relatives, and business associates. You can have at your fingertips any type of information that needs organizing. You can also automatically dial the telephone with Notebook as long as you have a modem. **Steps 17–20** cover the Notebook.

Up & Running with WordPerfect Library/Office PC covers Office PC, version 3.0, for IBM PC, PS/2, XT, AT, and compatibles running under DOS 2.1 or later. I recommend that the program be installed on a hard-disk drive, although you can run it from floppy-disk drives.

When you have worked your way through all 20 steps, you will be able to effectively use the programs that come with Office PC 3.0. I think you will be impressed at the organizational effectiveness of Office PC and make it a part of your everyday computing.

Enjoy!

—Jeff Woodward, September 1990

Table of Contents

Step 1
Installing Office PC   1

Step 2
Starting the Office PC Shell   5

Step 3
Working with the Shell   9

Step 4
Programming
the Office PC Shell   15

Step 5
Customizing the Shell   23

Step 6
Transferring Text
with the Clipboard   27

Step 7
Using the
Arithmetic Calculator   31

Step 8
Working with
the Calculator Tape   39

Step 9
Financial &
Scientific Calculators   45

Step 10
Statistical &
Programmer Calculators   55

Step 11
Starting the Calendar   61

Step 12
Organizing
with the Calendar   67

Step 13
Additional
Calendar Options   77

Step 14
Printing
with the Calendar   85

Step 15
Managing
Files with File Manager   91

Step 16
Managing Directories
with File Manager   99

Step 17
Organizing Your Desktop
with the Notebook   105

Step 18
Sorting & Printing
with the Notebook   115

Step 19
Creating a
New Notebook File   119

Step 20
Using Your Modem
with the Notebook   129

Installing Office PC

As with any other software package you've ever dealt with, you must prepare Office PC to run on your computer. This step guides you through a series of simple installation procedures that allow you to get up and running in just a few minutes.

Office PC is designed for use on a hard disk, and it is not recommended for use on a floppy-disk computer. You can install Office PC onto floppy disks, but you will have to do a great deal of disk swapping when using the various program utilities. This book deals only with installation to a hard disk.

The Office PC program files are stored in a compressed format that requires you to use the Office PC installation program, and you cannot run Office PC without first decompressing these files. You will need at least 2 Mb of free disk space to install Office PC.

Installing Office PC on a Hard Disk

You must run the Install program to install Office PC on your hard disk. If your computer has a 5¼″ floppy-disk drive, you will have four program disks. If you have a 3½″ floppy-disk drive, you will have two program disks.

Install program

Turn on your computer and follow the instructions below. You should see the C:> prompt displayed on your screen.

Installing Office PC

1. Place the WordPerfect Office PC 1 disk into drive A.

2. Type **A:** and press ↵ to change to drive A.

3. Type **INSTALL** and press ↵ to start the Office PC installation program. You are asked if you want to continue with the installation procedure.

4. Press Y or ⏎. The Office PC Installation Options
    screen appears, as shown in Figure 1.1.

*Basic
installation*

For this initial installation, you will use the Basic Installation
option. The remaining options are used to install specific
file groups or to update previously installed versions of
WordPerfect Library or Office PC. If you are interested in
using Office 3.0 on a LAN (local-area network), you can
select option 5 for some helpful information.

5. Press 1 or B to select Basic Installation. Information
    about the three steps in the installation procedure is
    displayed on your screen. Read it carefully before
    moving on.

6. Press Y or ⏎ to continue. Follow the instructions dis-
    played on your screen. You can now enter a different
    name for the Office PC hard-disk directory, or accept
    the displayed name of OFFICE30.

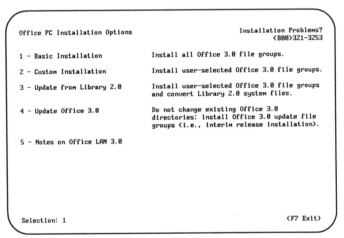

Figure 1.1: The Office PC Installation Options screen

If you elect to install Office PC on floppy disks, be sure you have available six double-density or two high-density 5¼" disks, or three low-density or two high-density 3½" blank, formatted disks onto which you will copy the decompressed program files.

Using floppies

7. Select option 3 to continue the installation. You will be prompted to insert the remaining program disks.

When the program asks for your registration number, it's a good idea to enter it, because you'll need it whenever you call for technical support or updates.

Registra- tion number

When you are asked to create or modify your AUTO-EXEC.BAT and CONFIG.SYS files, you should elect to do so to improve the operation of Office PC on your system. Follow the screen instructions carefully, and the Install program will automatically accomplish these tasks for you. If you want to modify or create an AUTOEXEC.BAT file yourself, refer to **Step 2.**

You will also be asked if you wish to install the Repeat Performance program. Since this is an entry-level book, you will not install this program now. Should you wish to do so, refer to the information in Appendix I, page 702, in your Office PC documentation.

8. Press N to skip the Repeat Performance installation and read the information about rebooting your computer. (You can press Ctrl-Alt-Del to reboot.)
9. Press any key to return to a DOS prompt. The installation of Office PC is complete.

Be sure to store your original WordPerfect Office PC disks in a safe location, free from excessive cold, heat, or dust, and away from appliances or equipment that produce electromagnetic energy.

Write
protection

Also, be sure to protect the disks from being accidentally overwritten. To do so, place a tab over the write-protect notch on each 5¼″ disk. (This notch is located next to the label.) A set of write-protect tabs comes with each box of new floppy disks. To write-protect a 3½″ disk, slide the movable tab located in one corner of the disk so you can see through the hole that the tab covers.

Starting the Office PC Shell

The Office PC Shell program serves as a program integrator, allowing you to run all your programs by pressing a single key. The Shell works with the Office PC programs, compatible WordPerfect Corporation programs such as WordPerfect and DataPerfect, and many other non–shell-compatible programs.

You can start the Office PC Shell in two ways: from a DOS prompt and with an AUTOEXEC.BAT file. Let's look at both these methods.

Starting the Shell from DOS

This section guides you through the procedures for manually starting the Office PC Shell from DOS. It assumes you have a rudimentary understanding of DOS.

Starting from DOS prompt

1. Start your computer and change to the directory containing the Office PC program files. If you use a floppy-disk computer, replace the DOS disk in drive A with the disk containing the Office PC program.
2. At the A> or C> prompt, type **shell** and press ↵. The Shell menu appears (Figure 2.1).

You are now ready to use the Shell to run programs.

Starting the Shell with an AUTOEXEC.BAT File

If you want to save time starting the Office PC Shell, you must either create a new AUTOEXEC.BAT file, or edit the existing AUTOEXEC.BAT file. Then, when you start your computer, the Shell automatically starts.

Starting with AUTO-EXEC .BAT file

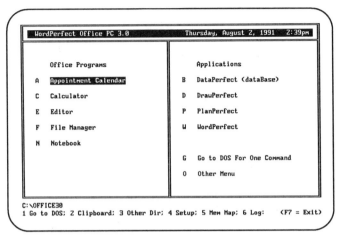

```
┌──────────────────────────────────────────────────────────────┐
│ WordPerfect Office PC 3.0          Thursday, August 2, 1991   2:39pm │
│ ┌──────────────────────────────┬──────────────────────────┐ │
│ │                              │                          │ │
│ │    Office Programs           │    Applications          │ │
│ │                              │                          │ │
│ │  A  Appointment Calendar     │  B  DataPerfect (dataBase)│ │
│ │                              │                          │ │
│ │  C  Calculator               │  D  DrawPerfect          │ │
│ │                              │                          │ │
│ │  E  Editor                   │  P  PlanPerfect          │ │
│ │                              │                          │ │
│ │  F  File Manager             │  W  WordPerfect          │ │
│ │                              │                          │ │
│ │  N  Notebook                 │                          │ │
│ │                              │  G  Go to DOS For One Command │ │
│ │                              │                          │ │
│ │                              │  O  Other Menu           │ │
│ │                              │                          │ │
│ └──────────────────────────────┴──────────────────────────┘ │
│ C:\OFFICE30                                                  │
│ 1 Go to DOS; 2 Clipboard; 3 Other Dir; 4 Setup; 5 Mem Map; 6 Log:   (F7 = Exit) │
└──────────────────────────────────────────────────────────────┘
```

Figure 2.1: The Shell menu

Using a text editor

The following sections show you how to create or edit an AUTOEXEC.BAT file using any *text editor* that can create or edit a DOS text file. A text editor is any program that allows you to type text and save it in DOS text format.

If you have WordPerfect, use the Text In/Out feature (Ctrl-F5, DOS Text) to retrieve, edit, and save your AUTOEXEC.BAT file.

To start your DOS text editor, press F7 to exit from the Shell. You are returned to a DOS prompt.

Existing AUTO-EXEC file

1. Start your DOS text editor. If you have an existing AUTOEXEC.BAT file, proceed with step 2. To create an AUTOEXEC.BAT file from scratch, skip step 2 and proceed with step 3.

2. Retrieve the existing AUTOEXEC.BAT file to the screen (Figure 2.2). If you use a floppy disk, place the

DOS disk containing your AUTOEXEC.BAT file in drive B.

3. Create or edit the AUTOEXEC.BAT path command to include all the directories that contain programs you want to start from the Shell menu. This is an example of a path command: *New AUTO-EXEC file*

    path=c:\;c:\wp51;c:\office30;c:\plan;c:\123

```
path=c:\;c:\wp51;c:\dos;c:\mouse;c:\pcplus;c:\123;c:\norton
prompt $p$g
cd \mouse
MOUSE
cls




C:\AUTOEXEC.BAT                              Doc 1 Pg 1 Ln 1" Pos 1"
```

Figure 2.2: A sample AUTOEXEC.BAT file

4. Enter the following three commands, each on a separate line, in the order shown.

cd\office30	Changes to OFFICE30 directory
cl/i	Allows Calendar alarms to work when using another program
shell	Starts Shell program; must be the last command in AUTOEXEC.BAT file

When you finish creating or editing the AUTOEXEC.BAT file, it should look similar to the one in Figure 2.3.

5.   Review your file entries, and then save the file as a DOS text file called AUTOEXEC.BAT.

6.   Press Ctrl-Alt-Del to reboot your computer. The program reads the new AUTOEXEC.BAT file, and the Office PC Shell menu appears on your screen, as shown in Figure 2.1.

In **Step 3**, you'll learn how to start programs from the Shell menu.

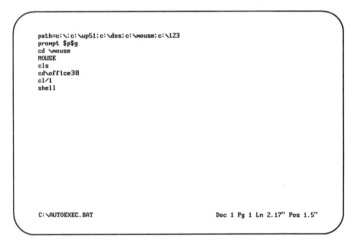

Figure 2.3: AUTOEXEC.BAT file with the Office PC commands

Working with the Shell

The Office PC Shell is a versatile program integrator. It offers several features that can assist you in your everyday computer tasks. This step will show you how to use the Shell to start your favorite programs and switch between them without exiting.

Starting Programs from the Shell Menu

The Shell menu, shown in **Step 2**, Figure 2.1, is the default menu. You'll notice that each program is assigned a Shell startup letter: *A* for Appointment Calendar, *C* for Calculator, and so on.

Shell menu

Although the Shell menu lists *Office Programs* and *Applications,* for simplicity's sake this book calls all of these items *programs*. In fact, you can even delete the Applications heading if you need more room to list the programs you use.

If you have installed Office PC on your hard disk, simply press the assigned menu letter for the program you want to run, and it starts. The Shell remains active in memory.

Running Shell programs

The F3 key activates the Shell Help feature. The Help screen displays helpful information for using the Shell.

If you run Office PC from a floppy disk, and want to run a program other than those included on the Office PC program disk, remove the Office PC disk from drive A and replace it with the appropriate program disk prior to pressing the menu letter assigned to that program. Refer to **Step 4** for information about assigning startup letters to new programs.

Using floppies

Moving between Programs

You won't be able to access an application until you install it on your hard disk and program it in the Shell menu (see **Step 4**).

The Office PC Shell allows you to run more than one program at the same time. This is useful when you want to refer to a document in another program, process a graphic image, or perform some file management operations without shutting down the program you're currently running.

Shelling Out to the Shell Menu

Shelling out with Ctrl-F1

Press the Shell key (Ctrl-F1) to temporarily exit from a WordPerfect Corporation program and return to the Shell. This procedure is called *shelling out*. Once you return to the Shell, you can run another program by pressing the appropriate startup letter. You can then press Ctrl-F1, shell out of that program to the Shell, and run yet another program.

If you start a program from the Shell menu that is *not* designed by WordPerfect Corporation, but has a Go to DOS command, you can press the appropriate keystrokes and temporarily shell out to the Shell.

Active (*) programs

When you shell out of a program, you see an asterisk (*) next to the program's assigned startup letter, as you can see in Figure 3.1. This reminds you that the program is running. In this example, the WordPerfect program is active.

Going to a DOS prompt

You can also shell out of the Shell menu to a DOS prompt. This is helpful when you want to use DOS, but you don't want to shut the Shell down.

Look at the menu options at the bottom of the Shell menu screen. To temporarily exit to DOS, press 1 (Go to DOS). You are presented with a DOS prompt with the word *shell* in parentheses in front of the DOS prompt to remind you the Shell is still active, as shown in Figure 3.2.

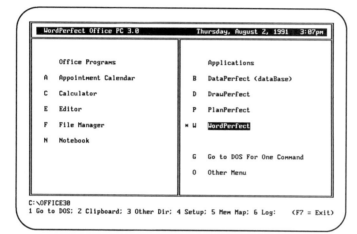

```
WordPerfect Office PC 3.0          Thursday, August 2, 1991   3:07pm


       Office Programs                    Applications

  A    Appointment Calendar         B     DataPerfect (dataBase)

  C    Calculator                   D     DrawPerfect

  E    Editor                       P     PlanPerfect

  F    File Manager               * W     WordPerfect

  N    Notebook

                                    G     Go to DOS For One Command

                                    O     Other Menu


C:\OFFICE30
1 Go to DOS; 2 Clipboard; 3 Other Dir; 4 Setup; 5 Mem Map; 6 Log:    (F7 = Exit)
```

Figure 3.1: Asterisks denote active programs

```
Enter the DOS command 'EXIT' (or Press F7) to return to the shell.

Microsoft(R) MS-DOS(R)  Version 3.30
             (C)Copyright Microsoft Corp 1981-1987

(shell) C:\OFFICE30>
```

Figure 3.2: The Shell reminder

To return to the Shell, either press F7, or type **exit** and press ⏎.

Switching Directly to Another Program

Switching to another program

You can also switch to another program without stopping at the Shell. All you need to know is the startup letter for the program you want to switch to. To switch immediately to another program, press Ctrl-Alt-*X*, where *X* is the *startup letter*. For example, if you are in WordPerfect, press Ctrl-Alt-A to start the Appointment Calendar. WordPerfect continues to run. You can do this with as many programs as will load into memory. When you no longer want a program active, exit from the program normally and return to the Shell menu.

Keeping Track of Memory Usage

Displaying available memory

The Shell can display the amount of memory currently in use by any program. To display the Shell Memory Map, press 5 (Mem Map) from the options at the bottom of the Shell menu screen, and you will see a screen similar to Figure 3.3. Press any key to return to the Shell menu.

(Unknown Name) listings

The Memory Map lists all the currently loaded programs and the amount of memory they occupy in bytes. Items listed as *(Unknown Name)* are programs or drivers to which the Shell cannot assign a name. The available memory and disk space are also displayed.

Expanded memory

The Shell is compatible with Lotus/Intel/MicroSoft (LIM) expanded memory specifications. When you shell out of a program with expanded memory in operation, you remove the program from conventional RAM and swap it into expanded memory. This frees up your available conventional memory for use by the next program you run. Figure 3.4 shows how the Memory Map indicates which programs are in expanded memory.

```
                 Memory Map

       Program Description      Memory Used

       1 DOS                       39968
       2 <Unknown Name)            11488
       3 Command                    3536
       4 Hsgrab                    23280
       5 Shell                     50144


       Available Memory:            526784
       Available Disk Space:       6799360




   <Press any key to return to the shell)
```

Figure 3.3: Memory Map screen

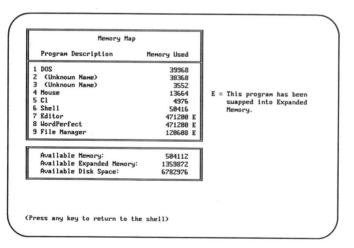

```
                 Memory Map

       Program Description      Memory Used

       1 DOS                       39968          E = This program has been
       2 <Unknown Name)            38368              swapped into Expanded
       3 <Unknown Name)             3552              Memory.
       4 Mouse                     13664
       5 Cl                         4976
       6 Shell                     50416
       7 Editor                   471200 E
       8 WordPerfect              471200 E
       9 File Manager             120608 E


       Available Memory:               504112
       Available Expanded Memory:     1359872
       Available Disk Space:         6782976



   <Press any key to return to the shell)
```

Figure 3.4: Programs swapped into expanded memory

Programming the Office PC Shell

By default, the Shell menu is programmed to start several shell-compatible utility programs. You can add or delete a program from the menu, or move a program from one location to another on the menu. In addition, you can edit existing program information. This step guides you through the procedures for adding, editing, deleting, and moving programs on the Shell menu.

Adding a Program to the Shell Menu

Adding a new program to the Shell menu is only a matter of a few quick steps.

1. Start your computer and run the Shell program.

2. Press 4 (Setup) from the Shell menu options displayed at the bottom of the screen. The Setup Menu appears, as shown in Figure 4.1.

The Setup Menu displays the names and assigned startup letters of programs, some of which are installed and ready for use. This menu includes items that are not installed. A menu line at the bottom of the screen displays several options that allow you to edit, add, delete, and move programs listed on the Setup Menu. The Options item (2) allows you to change screen colors, format the date and time, rename the menu title, establish a work log, set up the screen saver feature, specify a macro directory, select a password, and turn the Go to DOS option on and off.

Setup options

Several of the items on the Options menu are beyond the scope of this book. Refer to your Office PC documentation for an in-depth discussion of the advanced items not covered

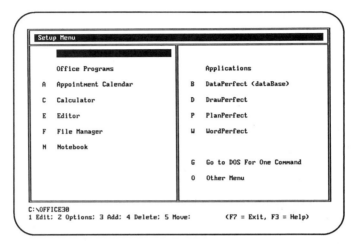

```
  Setup Menu

          Office Programs              Applications

     A  Appointment Calendar      B  DataPerfect (dataBase)

     C  Calculator                D  DrawPerfect

     E  Editor                    P  PlanPerfect

     F  File Manager              W  WordPerfect

     N  Notebook
                                  G  Go to DOS For One Command

                                  O  Other Menu


  C:\OFFICE30
  1 Edit; 2 Options; 3 Add; 4 Delete; 5 Move:        (F7 = Exit, F3 = Help)
```

Figure 4.1: The Setup Menu

here. Specifically, options 4 through 8 will not be discussed in this book.

3. Use the cursor keys to move the highlight to an empty program slot, where you'll add a new program.

If you want to insert a blank slot between existing program names, move the highlight to the slot where you want the new program name to appear and press 3 (Add). Program names on and below that slot will move downward one slot. See instructions in the next section.

4. Press 1, or ↵ (Edit) to display the Program Information screen, shown in Figure 4.2.

5. Type the menu letter that will start the new program. The highlight moves to the Menu Description line.

6. Type the name that you want to appear on the Shell menu.

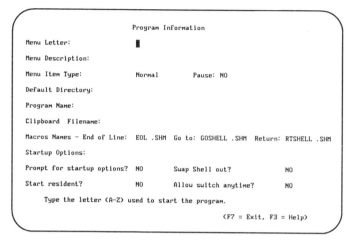

Figure 4.2: The Program Information screen

7. Place the highlight on the Program Name line, and type
    the name of the program file that starts the program.
    For example, to start Lotus 1-2-3 you would type
    123.EXE, as shown in Figure 4.3.

To learn about the rest of the items in the Program Information screen, see your Office PC documentation.

If you do not have a proper directory path entered in your
AUTOEXEC.BAT file, the program will not run. You will
need to type the full path name for the program file, including
drive and directory, on the Program Name line. For example,
the path for the program file shown in Figure 4.3 could be
c:\123\123.exe.

8. Press F7 twice to return to the Shell menu, where you
    can start the new program.

```
                    Program Information

Menu Letter:            L

Menu Description:       Lotus 1-2-3

Menu Item Type:         Normal        Pause: NO

Default Directory:

Program Name:           123.EXE

Clipboard  Filename:

Macros Names - End of Line:  EOL .SHM  Go to: GOSHELL .SHM  Return: RTSHELL .SHM

Startup Options:

Prompt for startup options?  NO        Swap Shell out?          NO

Start resident?              NO        Allow switch anytime?    NO

        Enter the name of the program.  You may include the full path
        for the program if it is found in another directory.
                                          (F7 = Exit, F3 = Help)
```

Figure 4.3: Program information for Lotus 1-2-3

Adding a Program to a Slot Occupied by Another Program

Follow this procedure when you want to place a new program name between two existing program names.

1. Select Setup from the Shell menu options.

2. Move the highlight to the slot where you want the new program name to appear.

3. Press 3 (Add) to add the new program. You can also press the Insert key.

All the programs from the new entry slot on down are moved downward one menu slot. As shown in Figure 4.4, the Notebook program was in the slot now occupied by the highlight. See the exercise later in this step for instructions about changing startup letters.

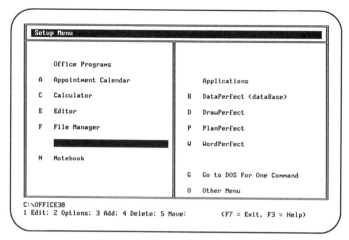

Figure 4.4: Inserting a new program

You cannot add a new program to any slot that has a program running in, or below, that slot. Nor can you add a new program if a program name occupies the last slot in the righthand column. You're also limited to the number of the programs that can fit on the screen.

4. Press 1 or ↵ (Edit) to display the Program Information screen.

5. Fill in the new program information. (Refer to the previous exercise.)

6. Press F7 twice to return to the Shell menu.

Deleting a Program from the Shell Menu

Deleting a program from the Shell menu is a quick and easy process.

You cannot delete a program from a slot that has a program running in, or below, that slot.

1. Select Setup from the Shell menu options.
2. Move the highlight to the program you want to delete.
3. Press 4 (Delete) or the Delete key. You are asked if you want to delete the entry from the Shell menu.
4. Press Y to delete, press N or ⏎ to prevent deletion.
5. Press F7 to return to the Shell menu. The programs below the deleted program move up one slot.

To prevent programs moving up a slot, place the highlight on the program to be deleted and press Ctrl-End (Delete to end of line). You are asked to confirm; press Y, and the program name disappears along with any program information.

Moving a Program

The Shell enables you to move an existing program from one menu location to another.

Moving a program to a slot occupied by another program deletes the existing program.

1. At the Shell menu, press 4 (Setup).
2. Move the highlight to the program you want to move.
3. Press 5 (Move). You are asked to type in the startup menu letter of the new location.
4. Press the startup letter of the new location. You are offered three options: 1 Move; 2 Copy; 3 Swap. Press 1 or M to move the program to the new slot. Press 2 or C to create a second copy of the program in the new slot.

Press 3 or S to trade places with a program existing in the new slot.

5. Press F7 to return to the Shell menu.

Changing a Startup Letter

Another organizational feature of Office PC is the ability to change an existing startup letter.

1. At the Shell menu, press 4 (Setup).

2. Move the highlight to the Shell entry where you want to change the startup letter.

3. Press 1 or ↵ (Edit). The cursor is located on the startup menu letter.

The new startup letter you choose must be an unused letter. If you select a letter that is in use, Office PC will overwrite that program, and you will lose it.

4. Type the new startup letter.

5. Press F7 twice to return to the Shell menu.

You can now start the program by pressing the newly assigned startup letter.

The next step provides pointers for customizing the Shell screen colors and changing the displayed date and time.

You can customize the Shell in several ways. You can change the colors of the screen display to achieve a more pleasing aesthetic effect or to improve the contrast. You can also change the format of the date and time displays. These next exercises introduce you to the options available to create a pleasing and efficient working environment.

Setting Screen Colors

If you have a color monitor, you will want to experiment with the different color combinations available with the Shell.

If you choose the wrong colors, some of your text may become invisible.

1. Press 4 (Setup) from the Shell menu options. The Setup Menu appears.
2. Press 2 (Options). The Options menu appears.
3. Press 1 or C (Colors). The Colors Setup screen, shown in Figure 5.1, appears.

The three options on the Color Setup screen tell the Shell what type of equipment you are using in your system. Selecting *Color monitor* will allow you to choose several different colors. Choosing *Single color monitor* (amber, green, or black-and-white) allows you to choose how underlining will be displayed: in reverse video or underlined. If you have a Hercules RamFont Card, and you are familiar with its operation, refer to the Office PC documentation for details about the available options.

Color Setup options

4. Select your monitor type.

```
                              Color Setup

          Monitor Characteristics:  0
             1 - Color monitor
             2 - Single color monitor (eg. Black & White or Compaq)
             3 - Hercules RamFont Card (InColor or Graphics Plus)
```

Figure 5.1: The Color Setup screen

Fast text display

You are asked if you want a fast text display. Pressing Y will speed up the time in which text is displayed on your screen. With some monitors, this can cause problems with the text display. Try both settings to see which works best with your monitor.

5. Press Y or N depending on your monitor capabilities. The color palette is displayed.

Selecting colors

You can choose between eight background colors represented by letters A through H, and sixteen foreground colors represented by letters A through P.

Use the ↑ and ↓ keys to move the cursor to each item. As you select a new color, the sample text demonstrates how your color choice will affect the normal screen. The colors you select will be used by all the Office PC programs, unless you select new colors from within each program.

6. Make your color selections.

7. Press F7 three times to return to the Shell menu. (If you decide not to accept the changes, press F1 to cancel, prior to pressing F7.)

Selecting a New Date/Time Format

The Shell options allow you to change the format for the date and time display. You can display the month and day in full or abbreviated text, or with numbers separated by slashes. The time can be displayed in 24-hour or 12-hour format. You can configure the date/time format in various ways, so I suggest you experiment with several formats until you find the one that works best for you.

Date/time format

1. Press 4 (Setup) from the Shell menu options.

2. Press 2 (Options).

3. Press 2 or D (Date/Time fmt). The Date Format screen, shown in Figure 5.2, appears.

```
Date Format

Number  Meaning
  1       Day of the month
  2       Month (number)
  3       Month (word)
  4       Year (all four digits)
  5       Year (last two digits)
  6       Day of the week (word)
  7       Hour (24 Hour Clock)
  8       Hour (12 Hour Clock)
  9       Minute
  0       am / pm
  %       Include leading zero on numbers less than 10
             (Must directly precede number)

Examples: 3 1, 4   = January 15, 1991
          2/1/5 (6) = 1/15/91 (Tuesday)
          8:90      = 10:13am

Date format: 6, 3 1, 4   8:90
```

Figure 5.2: The Date Format screen

Current date format

The current date format appears at the bottom of your screen. Each item of the current date and the time is represented by a number from the first column. Following each of these format numbers is a brief description of how the number translates into an actual date and time representation.

Limit the date/time format to 21 characters.

You can use punctuation marks, spaces, and letters along with the date/time numbers to create descriptive date/time formats. For example, entering

```
Hello! 6, 3 1, 4 8:90
```

Date/time format variations

will result in the Shell menu displaying

```
Hello! Tuesday, March 12, 1991 10:21 a.m.
```

4. Type the text and date format numbers.

5. Press F7 three times to return to the Shell menu. The new format will appear in the upper right corner of the Shell menu.

Transferring Text with the Clipboard

The Clipboard allows you to move existing text from one program into another. The Clipboard stores the text in a temporary buffer that holds up to 1K of data. This section demonstrates how to move text between shell-compatible programs (those made by WordPerfect Corporation) and non–shell-compatible programs.

Moving Text between Shell-Compatible Programs

You can transfer the following types of text with the Clipboard when using the four Office PC programs discussed in this book:

Program	Transferable Text
Calculator	Contents of the tape and display register
Calendar	Memos, appointments, and to-do list items
File Manager	Files
Notebook	Records, fields, and list displays

Transfer-ring text

You will find additional information on using the Clipboard with these programs in **Steps 7, 11, 16,** and **17.**

The following steps guide you through the procedure for using the Clipboard with WordPerfect Corporation programs other than those included with Office PC. These programs include WordPerfect, DataPerfect, and PlanPerfect.

1. From the Office PC Shell, start the program (WordPerfect, for example).

2. Press Alt-F4 and block-mark a section of text.

3. Press Ctrl-F1 (Shell).

The following Clipboard menu options appear at the bottom of your editing screen:

Clipboard menu options

Option	Action
Save	Saves the selected text to the Clip board buffer.
Append	Appends the selected text to the end of text already stored in the Clipboard buffer.
Retrieve	Retrieves text stored in the Clipboard buffer.
DOS Command	Allows you to execute a DOS command without exiting from the program.

4. Press 2 or S (Save). The text block is stored in the Clipboard buffer.

5. Hold down Ctrl-Alt as you press the menu letter for the shell-compatible program into which you want to place the copied text. The program starts.

6. Press Ctrl-F1 (Shell) to display the Clipboard menu options.

7. Press 2 or R (Retrieve) to retrieve the text stored in the Clipboard buffer.

Moving Text between Non–Shell-Compatible Programs

Screen Copy

The Clipboard uses a feature called *Screen Copy* to move text from a non–shell-compatible program into another program.

With Screen Copy, you can store all or part of the text displayed on your screen in the Clipboard buffer. Then, you can import the text into a shell-compatible or non–shell-compatible program. You press Alt-Shift--(hyphen) to activate the Screen Copy feature. You press Alt-Shift-+(plus) to retrieve stored data into a document.

Importing text

Be sure to use the hyphen and plus keys on the main keyboard, not the gray keys on the numeric keypad. The gray keys do not work.

Follow these steps to copy text with the Screen Copy feature.

1. From the Shell menu (or you can shell out to DOS), start the non–shell-compatible program.

2. Place some text on the screen.

3. Press Alt-Shift--(hyphen). The following Screen Copy options appear at the bottom of your screen: 1 Rectangle; 2 Block.

4. Select Rectangle to copy blocks of data that exist in a rectangular area on your screen, or select Block to copy blocks of data shaped in irregular patterns, similar to the way the Block command works in WordPerfect. Notice the cursor has become larger in size. This tells you the Block or Rectangle mode is operating.

Moving blocks or rectangles

Enlarged cursor

5. Use the arrow keys to move the enlarged cursor to the first letter of the first line of text you want to move.

6. Press ↵ to anchor the cursor at this location. The cursor expands to an even larger size.

7. Press the arrow keys to move the cursor over the text to be moved. The text is highlighted.

8. Press ↵. You will see the following options:

Option	*Action*
Save	Saves the blocked information in the Clipboard buffer.
Append	Appends the blocked information onto information already stored in the Clipboard buffer.
Format	Inserts a hard return, soft return, or merge return at the end of each line of blocked text.
Macro Variable	An advanced feature beyond the scope of this book.

9. Press 1 or S (Save) to save the text to the Clipboard buffer.

10. Start the program you want to move the text into.

11. Press Alt-Shift-+ to retrieve the text from the Clipboard buffer.

Using the Arithmetic Calculator

This step introduces you to the basic math features of the Calculator. In addition to an arithmetic calculator, the Calculator also provides four advanced calculators for scientific, programmer, financial, and statistical calculations (see **Steps 8** and **9**).

Starting the Calculator

The easiest method for starting the Calculator is to press the assigned Shell menu startup letter. You can, however, start the Calculator from a DOS prompt. Change to the OFFICE30 directory, type **calc**, and press ↵. The Calculator screen is shown in Figure 7.1. The two program files needed to run the Calculator are CALC.EXE and CALC.HLP.

Calculator screen

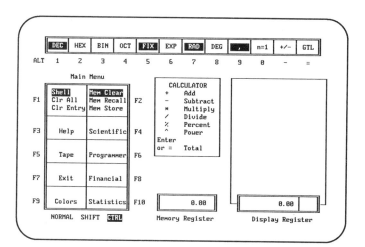

Figure 7.1: Calculator screen

The Calculator screen is organized into five areas:

- Main Menu

- Alt menu

- Help list of mathematical operators

- Memory Register

- Display Register and Tape

Varying the Numerical Display

Alt menu

The *Alt menu* is displayed across the top of the Calculator screen. On the Alt menu you can select from several types of numerical notations. Several of these notations are used with the advanced calculators. Table 7.1 outlines each type of notation.

Name	Key	Description
DEC	Alt-1	Decimal; floating decimal point
HEX	Alt-2	Hexadecimal (base 16)
BIN	Alt-3	Binary (base 2)
OCT	Alt-4	Octal (base 8)
FIX	Alt-5	Fixed; fixed decimal point (used with DEC only)
EXP	Alt-6	Exponential; for example, 2.23317+07

Table 7.1: Types of Numerical Notations

Performing Arithmetic Calculations

Entering numbers

The Calculator is ready to perform calculations as soon as you start it. You can enter numbers either with the number keys along the top row of your keyboard, or, if the Num Lock key is toggled on, from the numeric keyboard. You can enter up to ten numbers in the *Display Register*, located in the lower right corner of the Calculator screen. Numbers with more than seven digits are displayed as an exponent. For example, the number 220005000 is displayed as 2.20005+08.

Display Register

The arithmetic calculator performs addition, subtraction, multiplication, division, percentages, and exponentiation. The keys you press to activate these operators are listed in the box labeled *CALCULATOR* in the center of the Calculator screen.

CALCU-LATOR box

Directly above the display register is the *tape*. A running record of numerical entries is recorded on the tape.

Running record

The following exercises demonstrate how to enter each of the arithmetic operators when performing a calculation. First, let's calculate an example using the subtraction (negative), addition, division, and multiplication operators:

　　-200+350÷15x2=

1. Type **-200** (press the hyphen key or the minus key on the numeric keyboard to enter the negative sign).

2. Type **+350**.
3. Type **/15**.
4. Type ***2**.
5. Press ↵ or = (equal key) to display the answer of 20.

Now, let's raise the number 20 to the second power, which is the same as squaring it.

6. Press ^ (Shift-6) and type **2**.
7. Press ↵ to display the answer of 400.

Finally, let's determine 25 percent of 400.

8. Press *, type **25**, and press % (Shift-5). The answer of 100 appears.

Your screen should look like the one in Figure 7.2. The mathematical operators appear next to each entry.

Getting Help

The Main Menu for the Calculator is displayed on the left side of the Calculator screen. You can refer to the Main Menu for help in remembering the keystrokes needed to work with the arithmetic calculator and to activate the four advanced calculators. You will learn more about these calculators in **Steps 8** and **9**.

Help key
(F3)

To get help fast, press F3 (Help) to obtain information on the use of any key that has been assigned a Calculator function (see Figure 7.3). After you press F3, press the keystrokes for the function you need help with. For example, to receive help for clearing the Display Register, you press F3 followed by Shift-F1. To exit from Help, press the spacebar.

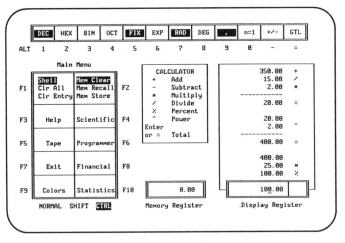

Figure 7.2: Using the arithmetic calculator

```
                                              CALC 3.0
Help Key

Use the Help key (F3) to get help or when you want information about
Calculator.  You may also press ? at any time to get help.

After pressing Help, you may press

      Any function key     to get help about that function.

      Any other key        to get information about how that key is used.

      Space Bar            to return to the Calculator.




  × Press the function key you need help for ×
```

Figure 7.3: The Help screen

Clearing the Display Register

Clear Entry (F1) and *Clear All* (Shift-F1) are used to clear the Display Register of numerical entries. The Clear Entry key clears the latest entry in the Display Register before you press Enter without ending the calculation. The Clear All key clears the Display Register and ends the calculation.

Clear Entry (F1)

Clear All (Shift-F1)

Using the Clipboard with the Display Register

The Clipboard feature lets you move a number from the Display Register into another document.

1. Type a number in the Display Register.

2. Press Ctrl-F1. The Clipboard options appear at the bottom of your screen.

3. Press 2 or S (Save to clipboard) to save the number to the Clipboard buffer. Press 3 or A (Append to clipboard) to append the number to the data currently stored in the Clipboard buffer.

The Clipboard is not available when using the Calculator from the DOS prompt.

Working with Values in Memory

Memory Register

The Calculator's *Memory Register* is located in the lower center of the Calculator screen. You can move a number in the Display Register to the Memory Register for use later. You can recall a number stored in the Memory Register to the Display Register when needed. You can also erase the number stored in the Memory Register.

1. To place a number in the Memory Register, type the number in the Display Register and press F2 (Mem Store).

2. To recall the number from the Memory Register and place it in the Display Register, first clear the Display Register by pressing F1, then press Shift-F2 (Mem Recall).

3. To erase the number in the Memory Register, press Ctrl-F2 (Mem Clear).

Calculating Grand Totals

Subtotals

At times, you will calculate several groups of numbers, each having its own total. These totals are called *subtotals*. The Calculator allows you to add all these subtotals to arrive at a grand total.

1. First, calculate the subtotals for each group of numbers.

2. Press Alt-= and the calculator will add the subtotals, creating a grand total. The letter *T* appears on the tape after a grand total (Figure 7.4).

Grand total with Alt-=

Setting Temporary Screen Colors

The Colors key (F9), also listed on the Main Menu, allows you to temporarily select colors different than those selected for the Shell. However, newly selected colors will only be in effect while the Calculator is operating. When you exit from and restart the Calculator, the colors established for the Shell will once again be in effect. To set temporary colors, press F9. To set permanent colors in the Calculator, see the Macros section in your manual. Refer to the instructions for selecting colors in **Step 5**.

Colors key (F9)

Step 8 guides you through the many ways of working with the Calculator tape.

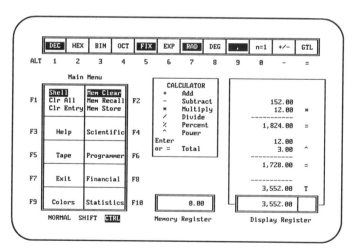

Figure 7.4: Calculating a grand total

Working with the Calculator Tape

15

The Calculator tape maintains a record of numerical entries, totals, subtotals, and grand totals for all your calculations. You press F5 (Tape) to display the seven options you can use when working with the Calculator tape. Let's look at some of the tasks these options perform.

Tape key (F5)

Turning the Tape On and Off

Sometimes you do not want entries placed in the Display Register to be recorded on the tape. For example, you can do supplemental calculations and not have those numerical entries appear on the tape along with the primary calculations.

In the following exercise, you will use the first Tape option to turn the tape on or off.

1. To display the Tape options, press F5 (Tape). The Tape options appear at the bottom of your screen (Figure 8.1).

2. Press 1 or T to select the first option.

3. Press N to turn the tape off. Press Y to turn the tape on.

Erasing the Tape

When you no longer need to keep a record of the numerical entries on the tape, you can erase them permanently.

Clearing the tape

1. Press F5 to see the Tape options.

2. Press 2 or C (Clear). The tape entries disappear.

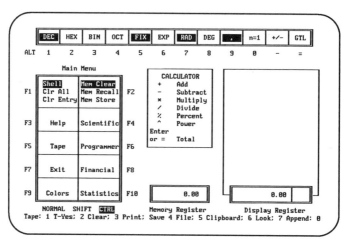

Figure 8.1: The Tape options

Printing the Contents of the Tape

*Printing
the tape*

You can print a copy of the numerical entries recorded on the Calculator tape.

1.   Turn on your printer.

2.   Press F5 to see the Tape options.

3.   Press 3 or P (Print). The following Print options appear on the bottom of your screen: 1 Print; 2 Select Print Device.

4.   Press 1 or P (Print) to print the tape contents. Press 2 or S (Select Print Device) to select a different parallel port (LPT1, LPT2, or LPT3), or to print the tape to a file for export to another computer.

Saving the Tape as a File

The tape can also be saved to disk as a DOS text file.

1. Press F5 to see the Tape options.

2. Press 4 or F to select the File option.

3. Type the file name. Include a path to save the file in a specific directory.

4. Press ↵. The tape is saved.

Using the Clipboard with the Tape

You can store the tape data in the Clipboard for importing into other programs. For a detailed discussion about how to use the Clipboard, refer to **Step 5.**

1. Press F5 to see the Tape options.

2. Press 5 or b (Clipboard) to store the tape contents in the Clipboard buffer (the existing data in the Clipboard will be replaced by this new number). Press 7 or A (Append) to append the tape contents to the data currently stored in the Clipboard buffer.

Using the Look Option

If you make many numerical entries, the list of numbers will scroll off the top of the tape display. To see these disappearing numbers, use the Look option. This option also allows you to place a number from the tape into the Memory and/or Display Register.

Scrolling through the Tape

You can use the Look option to view all the numerical entries on the tape.

1. Press F5 to see the Tape options.

2. Press 6 or L (Look). The first entry in the tape appears next to a small pointer (Figure 8.2).

3. Press ↑ or ↓ to scroll through the tape.

4. Press F7 to exit from Look mode.

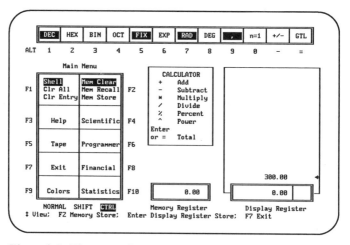

Figure 8.2: The tape pointer

Placing a Tape Entry into the Memory or Display Register

Moving a number

You can also move a number recorded on the tape into the Memory or Display Register.

1. Press F5 to see the Tape options.

2. Press 6 or L (Look).

3. Press ↑ or ↓ to place a number next to the pointer.

4. Press F2 (Memory Store) to place the entry into the
   Memory Register, or press ↵ to place the entry into the
   Display Register.

Step 9 introduces you to the basic functions available with
the Financial and Scientific Calculators.

Financial & Scientific Calculators

15

The Office PC Calculator includes four advanced calculators: Scientific, Programmer, Financial, and Statistics. In this step, you will learn the basic procedures for using the Financial and Scientific Calculators. You will be quite surprised at how quickly you can use these procedures in your own mathematical calculations.

Key Functions

The *Key Function* box in the center of each advanced calculator screen lists special keys for working with the calculator tape, quitting the calculator, getting on-screen help, and returning to the arithmetic calculator.

Key Function box

If you want to return to the arithmetic calculator, press Escape (Esc). If you want to exit from the Calculator completely and return to the Shell menu, press Ctrl-Q.

Exiting from calculators

To review the procedures for using the Tape (^T) and Help (?) functions, refer to **Step 7**. The ^ (caret) means press the Ctrl key and hold it down while pressing the T or Q key to select Tape or Quit.

Financial Functions

The Financial Calculator is useful for calculating profit margins, annuities, interest rates and costs, future and present values, principal amounts, product costs, and selling prices. These exercises only discuss the basics of using the Financial Calculator.

You'll notice the Financial Calculator is listed on the Main Menu of the arithmetic calculator. To activate the Financial

Financial Calculator (F8)

Calculator, press F8. You will see the Financial Calculator screen shown in Figure 9.1.

The Financial Functions menu is on the left side of the screen. The F1 and F2 function keys, in combination with the Shift and Ctrl keys, perform the same functions as on the Main Menu of the arithmetic calculator (see **Step 7**). The remaining function keys, F3 through F10, perform financial functions.

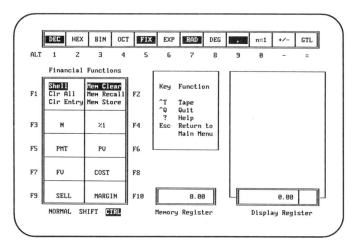

Figure 9.1: Financial Calculator screen

Table 9.1 describes the usage of each financial function.

Financial functions

Key	Function	Usage
F3	N	Type the time period and press F3.
F4	%i	Type the interest number and press F4 to determine the interest rate.

Table 9.1: The Financial Functions

Key	Function	Usage
F5	PMT	Type the payment amount and press F5.
F6	PV	Type the number for the principal amount or present value and press F6.
F7	FV	Type the number for the future value and press F7.
F8	COST	Type the number for the cost of the product and press F8.
F9	SELL	Type the number for the selling price and press F9.
F10	MARGIN	Type the number for the profit margin percentage (based on selling price) and press F10.

Table 9.1: The Financial Functions (continued)

Calculating Annuities

The Financial Calculator is useful for computing annuities of all types. An annuity is a series of payments made according to a regular, or fixed, payment schedule. A few examples of annuities are loans, mortgages, and retirement benefits.

Periodic payments

When you calculate annuities, use the PV (present value) or FV (future value) function in conjunction with the %i (percent interest), PMT (payment), and N (time) functions. Knowing any three of these items allows you to determine the fourth.

The Financial Calculator computes *ordinary annuities* (payments due at the end of a payment period). You can easily convert ordinary annuities to *annuities due* (payments due at the beginning of a payment period).

Types of annuities

Calculating an Ordinary Annuity

Using functions

To use the Financial Calculator, you first type a number into the Display Register. Then, you assign a financial function to the entered number by pressing the appropriate function key.

Monthly loan payment

The following example demonstrates the procedure for calculating a monthly loan payment, which is an example of an ordinary annuity. The known variables are loan amount (PV), time period in months (N), and interest rate (%i). The unknown variable is the monthly payment (PMT).

1. From the arithmetic calculator, press F8 to start the Financial Calculator.

2. Enter **14,800** as the loan amount and press F6 (PV).

3. Enter **11** as the annual interest rate and divide it by 12 to determine the amount of interest per month. Then, press F4 (%i).

4. Enter **60** as the time period (in months) for the loan payments and press F3 (N).

5. Press Shift-F5 to calculate the monthly payment (PMT). Figure 9.2 shows the result of this calculation: **321.79** is the monthly loan payment. Notice that the tape records *PV, %i, N,* and *PMT* next to each corresponding entry.

Calculating an Annuity Due

Annuity due

You can use two methods for converting an ordinary annuity to an annuity due. If you calculate PV or FV, *multiply* the result by a factor of

    (1+i)

where *i* is the periodic interest rate expressed as a decimal. If you calculate PMT or N, *divide* PV or FV by

`(1+i)`

and use this value with the other known values to calculate the annuity due.

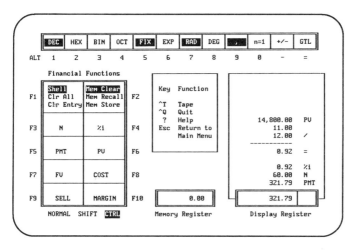

Figure 9.2: Calculating a monthly loan payment

Calculating Interest

You can also use the Financial Calculator to compute simple and compound interest. The following example is a guide for calculating the amount of compound interest that will accrue on a hypothetical savings account. The known variables are starting balance (PV), interest rate compounded monthly (i), and time period (N). The unknown variable is the future value (FV).

1. With the Financial Calculator displayed on your screen, enter the starting balance and press F6 (PV).

Calculating compound interest

2. Enter the annual interest rate and divide by 12, since the interest is compounded monthly.

3. Press F4 (%i) to enter the computed monthly interest rate.

4. Enter the total number of months in the time period and press F3 (N).

5. Press Shift-F7 (Calculate future value) to calculate the amount of savings at the end of the known period.

The time entries in steps 2 and 4 above must be based on the same periods. For example, if you use months in step 2, then the total number of months should be used in step 4. If you use years in step 2, then don't divide the interest rate by 12; instead, use the total years in step 4.

Calculating Profit Margins

For the final exercise with the Financial Calculator, let's go through the steps for computing the profit margin when you buy an item at one price and sell it at a higher price. For this type of problem, you use the Cost (F8), Sell (F9), and Margin (F10) function keys. Knowing any two of these variables allows you to calculate the remaining variable. In the following example, the known variables are cost (COST) and selling price (SELL). The unknown variable is profit margin (MARGIN).

Calculating a profit margin

1. From the Financial Calculator screen, press Shift-F1 to clear the Display Register.

2. Enter the cost and press F8 (COST).

3. Enter the selling price and press F9 (SELL).

4. Press Shift-F10 to calculate the profit margin.

Scientific Functions

The Scientific Calculator is used to compute scientific functions. These functions are organized into three types: general functions, logarithmic and exponential functions, and trigonometric functions.

To start the Scientific Calculator, you must have the arithmetic calculator displayed on your screen. You'll notice the Scientific Calculator is assigned the F4 function key on the Main Menu. Press F4 to display the Scientific Calculator screen (Figure 9.3).

Scientific Calculator (F4)

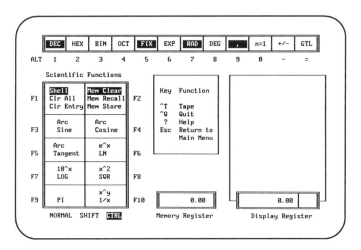

Figure 9.3: Scientific Calculator screen

The Scientific Functions menu is displayed at the left side of the Scientific Calculator screen. The F1 and F2 function keys, in combination with the Shift and Ctrl keys, perform the same functions as with the arithmetic calculator. The remaining function keys, F3 through F10, perform scientific functions.

General Scientific Functions

You can use the general scientific functions, summarized in Table 9.2, in various mathematical calculations.

General scientific functions

Key	Function	Usage
F8	SQR	Type a known value and press F8 to compute the square root of the known positive value
Shift-F8	x^2	Type the value x and press Shift-F8 to compute the square of the known value.
F9	PI (π)	Press F9 to display the value of pi in the Display Register (pi is accurate to ten decimal places).
F10	$1/x$	Type the value x and press F10 to compute the reciprocal of x.

Table 9.2: General Scientific Functions

The SQR function will not compute the square root of a negative number. You must enter a positive number.

Logarithmic and Exponential Functions

The logarithmic and exponential functions will greatly assist your engineering calculations. Table 9.3 summarizes these functions.

Logarithmic and exponential functions

Key	Function	Usage
F6	LN	Enter a known value and press F6 to compute the *natural log* (the base *e* logarithm) of the known value.

Table 9.3: Logarithmic and Exponential Functions

Key	Function	Usage
Shift-F6	e^x	Enter the value *x* and press Shift-F6 to compute the *natural antilog* (raise *e* to the power of *x*).
F7	LOG	Enter a known value and press F7 to compute the *common log* (the base 10 logarithm) of the known value.
Shift-F7	10^x	Enter the value *x* and press Shift-F7 to compute a *common antilog* (raise 10 to the power of *x*).
Shift-F10	x^y	Type the value *x* and press Shift-F10. Then, type the value *y*, and press ↵ to raise *x* to the power of *y*.

Table 9.3: Logarithmic and Exponential Functions (continued)

Trigonometric Functions

The trigonometric functions of the Scientific Calculator will assist you in your advanced calculations. Table 9.4 describes the usage for each function.

Key	Function	Usage
F3	Sine	Type the number of radians or degrees and press F3 to compute the sine.
Shift-F3	Arc Sine	Type the known value for the sine and press Shift-F3 to compute the angle in degrees or radians.

Trigono-metric functions

Table 9.4: Trigonometric Functions

Key	Function	Usage
F4	Cosine	Type the number of degrees or radians and press F4 to compute the cosine.
Shift-F4	Arc Cosine	Type the known value for the cosine and press Shift-F4 to compute the angle in degrees or radians.
F5	Tangent	Type the number of degrees or radians and press F5 to compute the tangent.
Shift-F5	Arc Tangent	Type the known value for the tangent and press Shift-F5 to compute the angle in degrees or radians.

Table 9.4: Trigonometric Functions (continued)

Radians vs. degrees

The Calculator, by default, measures an angle entered in the Display Register in radians. If you want the angle to be interpreted in degrees, press Alt-8 (DEG). To return to radians, press Alt-7 (RAD). The Alt menu at the top of your Calculator screen will reflect these changes.

Step 10 introduces you to the functions offered with the Statistical and Programmer Calculators.

Statistical & Programmer Calculators

This step covers the two remaining advanced calculators: Statistical and Programmer. This material is not designed to make you a statistical expert or a programmer; you must already be familiar with those disciplines before you can take advantage of the information presented here. You will, however, learn about the tools available with each of these advanced calculators.

Key Functions

The *Key Function* box in the center of each advanced calculator screen lists special keys for working with the calculator tape, quitting the calculator, getting on-screen help, and returning to the arithmetic calculator.

Key Function box

The procedures for using the Tape and Help functions are the same as those discussed in **Step 7**.

If you want to return to the arithmetic calculator, press Escape (Esc). If you want to exit from the Calculator completely and return to the Shell menu, press Ctrl-Q.

Exiting from calculators

The ^ (caret) symbol in front of the T and Q in the Key Function box means hold down the Ctrl key while pressing the T or Q key to select Tape or Quit.

Statistical Functions

If you work with groups of numbers to compute standard deviations, variances, or statistical calculations, you will find the Statistical Calculator useful. Eight functions are offered on the Statistical Functions menu on the left side of the Statistical Calculator.

*Statistical
Calculator
(F10)*

After you start the arithmetic calculator, press F10 on the Main Menu to display the Statistical Calculator screen shown in Figure 10.1.

The Statistical Functions menu is displayed on the left side of the screen. The F1 and F2 function keys, in combination with the Shift and Ctrl keys, perform the same functions as with the arithmetic calculator. The F3 through F10 function keys perform statistical functions.

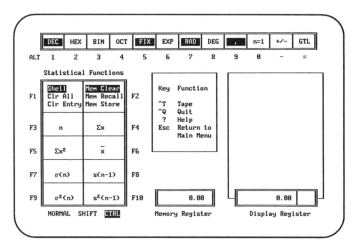

Figure 10.1: The Statistical Calculator screen

The statistical functions listed in Table 10.1 perform operations on groups of numbers. Therefore, before you activate a function, enter all the numbers, pressing ↵ after each entry.

Key	Function	Usage
F3	n	Press F3 to obtain a count of the number of entries.

*Statistical
functions*

Table 10.1: Statistical Functions

Key	Function	Usage
F4	Σx	Press F4 to obtain the sum of the numbers entered.
F5	Σx^2	Press F5 to compute the square of each entry and display the sum of the squared entries.
F6	$\bar{x}$	Press F6 to compute the average (arithmetic mean) of the numbers.
F7	$\sigma(n)$	Press F7 to compute the *population standard deviation* for a group.
F8	$s(n-1)$	Press F8 to compute the *sample standard deviation* for a group.
F9	$\sigma^2(n)$	Press F9 to compute the *population variance* for a group.
F10	$s^2(n-1)$	Press F10 to compute the *sample variance* for a group.

Table 10.1: Statistical Functions (continued)

Programmer Functions

Office PC provides a Programmer Calculator for those of you who like or need to do programming. You can perform operations such as shifting and rotating functions, working with complement functions, and two-variable functions. Fifteen functions are offered with the Programmer Calculator.

After you start the arithmetic calculator, you'll notice the Programmer Calculator is assigned the F6 function key on the Main Menu. Press F6 to display the Programmer Calculator screen (Figure 10.2).

Programmer Calculator (F6)

The Programmer Functions menu is displayed on the left side of the screen. The F1 and F2 function keys, in combination

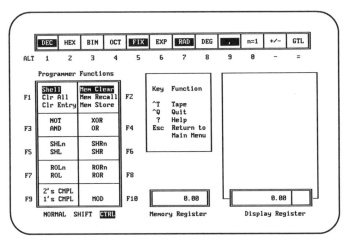

Figure 10.2: The Programmer Calculator screen

with the Shift and Ctrl keys, perform the same functions as with the arithmetic calculator. The F3 through F10 function keys, alone and in conjunction with the Shift key, perform programmer functions.

The Programmer Calculator presumes the number entered in the display register is a 32-bit integer when you use the OCT (Alt-4) and HEX (Alt-2) options.

The list in Table 10.2 describes how to use each programmer function. You first enter a number, then press the appropriate function key.

To set the value for *n* used in the shift and rotate functions, press Alt-0 and enter a number from 0 to 9 in the Alt menu at the top of the Programmer Calculator screen.

Key	Function	Usage
F3	AND	Type a number, press F3, type the second number, and press ↵ to compute the bitwise AND.
Shift-F3	NOT	Press Shift-F3 to return the 1's complement of a number.
F4	OR	Type a number, press F4, type the second number, and press ↵ to compute the bitwise inclusive OR.
Shift-F4	XOR	Type a number, press Shift-F4, type the second number, and press ↵ to compute the bitwise exclusive OR.
F5	SHL	Press F5 to shift a number one bit to the left.
Shift-F5	SHLn	Set the value for n, type a number, and press Shift-F5 to shift the number n bits to the left.
F6	SHR	Press F6 to shift a number one bit to the right.
Shift-F6	SHRn	Set the value for n, type a number, and press Shift-F6 to shift the number n bits to the right.
F7	ROL	Press F7 to rotate a number one bit to the left. The leftmost bit becomes the rightmost bit.
Shift-F7	ROLn	Set the value for n, type a number, and press Shift-F7 to rotate the number to the left n times.

Programmer functions

Table 10.2: Programmer Functions

Key	Function	Usage
F8	ROR	Press F8 to rotate a number one bit to the right.
Shift-F8	ROR*n*	Set the value for *n,* type a number, and press Shift-F8 to rotate the number to the right *n* times.
F9	1's CMPL	Press F9 to return the 1's complement of the number.
Shift-F9	2's CMPL	Press Shift-F9 to return the 2's complement of a number.
F10	MOD	Type a number, press F10, type the second number, and press Enter. The first number is divided by the second number, and the remainder is displayed in the display register.

Table 10.2: Programmer Functions (continued)

Starting the Calendar

 15

The Office PC Calendar is useful for scheduling important appointments, compiling and prioritizing to-do lists, and creating memos to remind you of significant events. On the opening screen, it is called the Appointment Calendar; elsewhere in the program, it is called the Calendar.

This step shows you how to start the Calendar and move between the three organizational tools provided with the program.

Starting the Calendar

You can start the Calendar in two ways (if Office PC is on your path or you're in the Office PC directory):

- From the Shell menu, press the startup menu letter that is assigned to the Calendar

- From a DOS prompt, type **CL** and press ↵

The Calendar screen is shown in Figure 11.1. The two program files that are needed to run the Calendar are CL.EXE and CALENDAR.HLP.

The left side of the Calendar screen displays an eight-week calendar with the current date shown in reverse video. You can display any date that falls between January 1, 1600, and December 31, 9999.

Calendar screen

The right side of the Calendar screen combines the Memo, Appointments, and To-Do List windows. You can place data into these windows for any date selected on the calendar (see **Step 12** to learn how to do this).

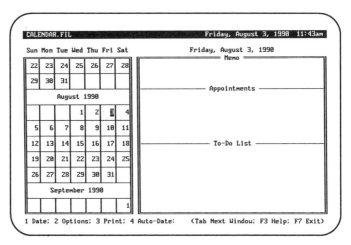

Figure 11.1: The Calendar screen

Appointments window

You can schedule appointments in the Appointments window according to specific times. You can also set the alarm to alert you to an impending appointment.

To-Do List window

You can enter personal tasks in the To-Do List window. You can also program the To-Do List to automatically move items not accomplished to the next calendar day.

Menu bar

At the bottom of the Calendar screen is a menu bar that allows you to select a specific date, customize certain calendar features, print the calendar entries, and schedule recurring calendar entries. Helpful hints are also provided for moving between the calendar windows, getting help, and exiting from the Calendar.

Help (F3)

The Calendar offers a context-sensitive Help feature that enables you to receive help from anywhere in the Calendar.

Press F3 to display a master menu listing all the topics for which help is available, as shown in Figure 11.2. You can obtain help by pressing any function key. Press F3 twice for the function-key template, or type any of the letters for the listed topics.

```
Help
    File: C:\HSG\CALENDAR.FIL                    CL 3.0


        Press any function key to get information about the use of the key.
        Press Help (F3) again to see a template for the function keys.
        Press the following letters to get information about specific topics:

        A - Movement in Calendar          N - Saving/Retrieving Calendars
        B - Entering Memos and Text       O - Starting/Exiting Calendar
        C - Entering Appts/Alarms         P - Startup Options
        D - Entering To-Do Lists          Q - Auto-Date Formula Entry
        E - Moving or Copying Text        R - Holiday Autodate Formulas
        F - Printing the Calendar         S - Date
        G - Date/Time Formats
        H - Alarm Options                 Y - Customer Support
        I - Appt/To-Do Options            Z - Extended Character Set
        J - Auto Archive/Delete/Backup Options
        K - Set Colors
        L - File Export Format/Password
        M - Scheduler File Paths


    A-Z Topic: 0              (ESC Topics; Space Exit; Function Key Help for Key)
```

Figure 11.2: The Calendar Help screen

Moving through the Calendar

You can move the calendar highlight to another date in the calendar in several ways. Table 11.1 shows you the cursor keys that move the highlight.

Moving to any date

Keys	Cursor Movement
Left Arrow *or* Page Up	Backward one day
Right Arrow *or* Page Down	Forward one day
Up Arrow	Backward one week
Down Arrow	Forward one week

Table 11.1: Cursor Keys for Moving the Calendar Highlight

Keys	Cursor Movement
– on the numeric keypad*	Backward one month
+ on the numeric keypad*	Forward one month
Home, Page Up	Backward one year
Home, Page Down	Forward one year
Ctrl-Home, Enter	Return to current date
*NumLock must be off	

Table 11.1: Cursor Keys for Moving the Calendar Highlight (continued)

Moving between Calendar windows

To place text in the Memo, Appointments, and To-Do List windows, you must move the highlight from the calendar into the appropriate window. To move clockwise through the windows, press Tab. To move counterclockwise, press Shift-Tab. When the calendar highlight moves into a window, it becomes a normal editing cursor.

Using the Clipboard with the Calendar

You can use the Clipboard to transfer information from the Calendar into another WordPerfect Corporation program. Refer to your WordPerfect Office Workbook for a detailed discussion of the Clipboard feature and of moving information between programs.

The following instructions show you how to save or append data to the Clipboard.

These instructions work only if you are within the Shell.

1. Move the calendar highlight to the appropriate date.

2. Press Tab to move the cursor into the Memo, Appointments, or To-Do List window.

3. Move the cursor to the memo, appointment, or to-do task to be copied.

4. Press Ctrl-F1 to display the Clipboard menu.

5. Press 2 or S (Save) to save the data, or press 3 or A (Append) to append the data to existing text in the Clipboard buffer.

To retrieve the Clipboard data from the clipboard buffer into another program, follow the next set of instructions.

These instructions work only if you are within the Shell.

1. Start the appropriate program and place the cursor where you want to insert the text.

2. Press Ctrl-F1 to display the Clipboard menu.

3. Press 4 or R (Retrieve) to retrieve the text from the Clipboard buffer.

Step 12 shows you how to enter data into the Memo, Appointments, and To-Do List windows.

Organizing with the Calendar

This step guides you through the procedures for entering and editing data in the Memo, Appointments, and To-Do List windows of the Calendar. To use these windows, start the Shell and select the Appointment Calendar.

Before you begin working with text placed in any of the three Calendar windows, you need to become familiar with a few editing function keys, listed in Table 12.1.

Key	Function	Usage
F2	Forward Search	Search forward through text for specific words or phrases.
Shift-F2	Backward Search	Search backward through text for specific words or phrases.
Shift-F7	Print	Print memos, appointments, and to-do lists.
Ctrl-F5	File Options	Export calendar data in Calendar 1.1 and 2.0/3.0 formats.
F1	Cancel	Restore deleted appointments and to-do entries.
Ctrl-F4	Cut	Move an item from one Calendar window to another.

Editing function keys

Table 12.1: Editing Function Keys

Key	Function	Usage
F4	Copy	Copy an item from one Calendar window to another.
Shift-F10	Retrieve/Paste	Place text that has been cut or copied from one Calendar window into another and retrieve calendar files.
F6	Bold	Print entered text in bold type.
F8	Underline	Print entered text with an underline.
F7	Exit	Exit from the Memo window.

Table 12.1: Editing Function Keys (continued)

Creating Memos

You can enter up to 255 characters in a memo. As you type text into the Memo window, it automatically wraps to the next line upon reaching the window boundary. You can also move the cursor to the next line by pressing ⌐.

To enter text into the Memo window, follow these steps:

1. Move the calendar highlight to the date for which you want the memo to apply.

2. Press Tab to move the Calendar highlight into the Memo window.

After you press Tab and move into the Memo window, you can press F3 to display the Help screen. You immediately receive a brief description of the function keys available for selecting text-editing features.

3. Type in the text. The size of the Memo window increases. Notice the menu line at the bottom of the screen (Figure 12.1).

4. Press F7, Tab, or Shift-Tab to exit from the Memo window and return to the calendar.

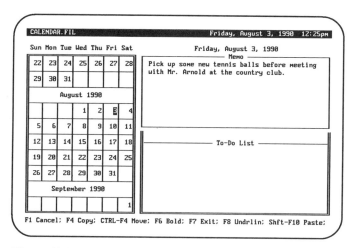

Figure 12.1: The Memo menu line

When you exit from any Calendar window, you see a small dot (·) beside the date on the calendar. This dot denotes an entry for that date. Move the calendar highlight to that date, and the entries will be displayed.

Scheduling Appointments with the Calendar

You can easily keep track of your daily appointments with the Appointments feature. You can enter an appointment for any time of the day. Each appointment description is limited to 255 characters. You can set an alarm to alert you of an impending appointment, adjust the appointment time if it changes, delete the appointment, or insert a new appointment.

Entering an Appointment

Follow these steps to enter an appointment:

1. Move the calendar highlight to the appointment date.

2. Press Tab twice to move into the Appointments window. Notice the menu line at the bottom of the screen (Figure 12.2).

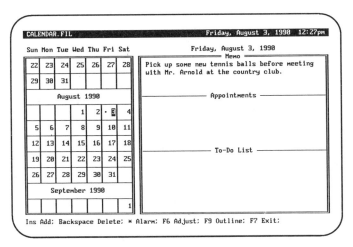

Figure 12.2: The Appointments menu line

You will see the options listed in Table 12.2 in the Appointments window menu line.

*Appoint-
ments
menu
options*

Key	Function	Usage
Ins	Insert	Add a new appointment.
Backspace	Backspace	Delete an existing appointment.

Table 12.2: Appointments Menu Options

Key	Function	Usage
*	Asterisk	Turn the alarm on or off.
F6	Adjust	Change an existing appointment time.
F9	Outline	Display an outline of hourly increments.
F7	Exit	Exit from the Appointments window (F7).

Table 12.2: Appointments Menu Options (continued)

3. Press Ins (Insert) to add a new appointment. You are prompted to enter the time of the appointment.

4. Type the time and press ↵.

If you enter time for a 12-hour clock, include an *a* for a.m. or a *p* for p.m. You can also enter time for a 24-hour clock (see **Step 13** for selecting 24-hour time).

12-hour clock

If you want to schedule an ending time for the appointment, press Tab and type in the time.

Ending time

5. Type the appointment description (up to 255 characters) and press F7. The appointment is scheduled.

6. Press * to turn the alarm on or off. Figure 12.3 shows an example of an appointment with the alarm turned on.

When an alarm rings, press Alt-spacebar to turn it off, or it will ring at a specified interval until the appointment time (see **Step 13**).

7. Press F7, Tab, or Shift-Tab to exit from the Appointments window.

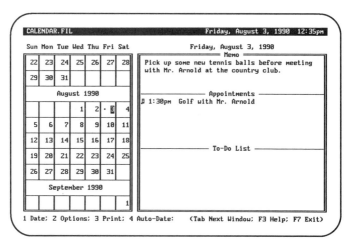

Figure 12.3: Appointment with the alarm turned on

Editing and Deleting an Appointment

These steps tell you how to reenter the Appointments window and delete or edit an appointment.

1. Move the calendar highlight to the appropriate date.

2. Press Tab twice to place the cursor in the Appointments window.

3. Move the cursor to the appointment you want.

4. To delete the appointment, press Backspace. To edit the appointment, press ⏎ and make the needed changes.

5. Press F7 twice to return the highlight to the calendar.

Restoring a Deleted Appointment

Have you ever canceled an appointment, only to have it rescheduled again? Well, if you use Backspace to delete an appointment, you can restore the appointment without inserting and retyping the appointment description again.

1. Press Tab to move to the Appointments window.

2. Press F1. The description of the last appointment you deleted is displayed on the bottom of your screen along with these prompts: 1 Restore; 2 Previous.

3. Press 1 or R (Restore) to restore the displayed appointment, or press 2 or P (Previous) to display the next-to-last deletion. The Calendar remembers the last two deletions you made.

Prioritizing Tasks with the To-Do List

You can enter important tasks in the To-Do List window in order of priority. Once a priority is assigned to a task, you can change the priority without retyping the task description. You can also have the Calendar automatically carry over to the next day those tasks not done.

Creating a To-Do List

To enter tasks into the To-Do List window, follow these instructions:

1. Move the calendar highlight to the date for the To-Do List tasks.

2. Press Tab three times to move to the To-Do List window. The To-Do List menu options appear at the bottom of the screen (Figure 12.4).

Key	*Function*	*Usage*
Ins	Insert	Add a new task to the list.
Backspace	Backspace	Delete an existing task from the list.

To-Do List options

Table 12.4: To-Do List Options

Key	Function	Usage
*	Asterisk	Mark a task that has been completed. Without the asterisk, the task will be carried forward to the next day.
F6	Adjust	Change the priority of an existing task.

Table 12.4: To-Do List Options (continued)

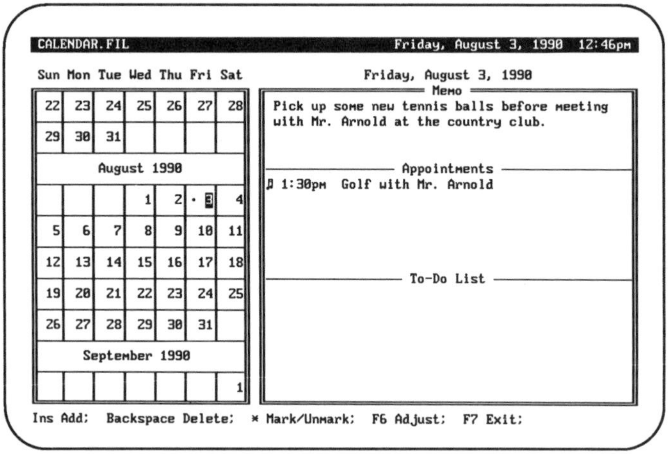

Figure 12.4: The To-Do List menu line

3. Press Insert (Ins) and, when prompted, type in a number for the priority of the task, and press ↵.

4. Type the description of the task (limit of 255 characters).

5. Press F7 twice to exit from the To-Do List window.

Editing and Deleting a To-Do List

The following steps instruct you in deleting and making changes to existing To-Do List items.

1. Select the calendar date you want and press Tab three times to move the cursor into the To-Do List window.

2. To delete a task, place the cursor on the task and press Backspace.

3. To edit a task, move the cursor to the task to be edited and press ↵ (the enlarged editing window appears).

4. Edit the text.

5. Press F7 twice to exit from the To-Do List window.

If you edit a task and then change your mind, press F1 to exit from the To-Do List without recording the changes.

Restoring a Deleted To-Do List Task

The restore feature is a lifesaver if you delete a To-Do List item by mistake. Text that you delete is stored in a temporary buffer from which you can retrieve it prior to exiting from the Calendar. The Calendar will remember the last two deletions you made from the To-Do List. If you delete a To-Do List item, and then wish to get it back, follow these steps:

1. Tab to move the cursor into the To-Do List window.

2. Press F1 (Cancel). At the bottom of your screen, you see a small amount of text from the most recently deleted item and the following prompt: 1 Restore; 2 Previous.

3. Press 1 or R (Restore) to retrieve the last deletion, or select Previous (press 2 or P) to restore the next-to-last deletion.

Step 13 teaches you how to customize the Calendar formats. You can select new colors, set alarms, and change the date and time format. You will also receive pointers on using the Clipboard and printing Calendar entries.

Additional Calendar Options

This step introduces you to some important Calendar options, including selecting new colors, setting alarms, scheduling memos, appointments, and to-do tasks on a regular basis, changing the date and time format, and exporting files in Calendar version 1.1 format. You also receive pointers on using the Clipboard and printing Calendar entries. These options are selected from the menu line at the bottom of the Calendar screen.

To use these features, start the Shell and enter the Calendar.

Working with the Date Option

The Date option allows you to move the calendar highlight to a specific date (Go to Date), forward or backward a specified number of days (Move Days), and calculates the number of days between two specified dates (Date Difference).

Date option

Moving to a Specified Date

The Go to Date option is handy for making large jumps over several days, weeks, months, or years. To use this option, follow these steps:

Go to Date option

1. Press 1 or D (Date).
2. Press 1 or G (Go to Date).
3. Type in the complete date (according to the format displayed in parentheses) and press ↵. The calendar highlight moves to that date.

To return to the current date from anywhere in the Calendar, select the Go to Date option and press ↵.

Moving a Specified Number of Days

Moving by number of days

The Move Days option allows you to position the calendar highlight a specified number of days forward or backward in the Calendar. Here's how it's done.

1. Press 1 or D (Date) to display the Date options.

2. Press 2 or M (Move Days).

3. Type the number of days you want to move forward and press ↲. To move backward, type a minus sign (or hyphen) in front of the number of days and press ↲. The highlight moves to the new date.

Calculating the Number of Days between Two Dates

Date Difference option

The Date Difference feature determines the number of days between two specified dates.

1. Move the calendar highlight to the first date.

2. Press 1 or D (Date).

3. Press 3 or D (Date Difference).

4. Type in the second date and press ↲. The number of days between the two dates is displayed at the bottom of your screen.

5. Press any key to return to the Calendar.

Working with the Calendar Setup Options

Setup options

You can customize the Calendar in various ways using the setup options. You can change the date/time format, set alarms, modify the way the Appointments and To-Do List work, save or delete old calendar entries, set new colors, and save calendar files in the Calendar 1.1 and 2.0/3.0 formats.

To select a setup option, press 2 or O (Options). The Setup Options menu appears, as shown in Figure 13.1.

Changing the Date/Time Formats

The date/time options change the way the date and time are displayed on the calendar, specify which day is the first day in the week, and reset your computer's internal clock for the correct time and date.

```
Setup Options

    1 - Date/Time Formats

    2 - Alarms

    3 - Appointments/To-Do

    4 - Archive/Delete/Backup

    5 - Colors

    6 - File Format




Selection: 0
```

Figure 13.1: The Setup Options menu

To change any one of these items, press 1 or D (Date/Time Formats). The Date/Time Formats screen will then be displayed (Figure 13.2).

Look over this screen carefully, for it tells you exactly how to enter the correct formatting characters. These characters determine how the date and time will be displayed. Notice the Date/Time Formats menu at the bottom of your screen.

Entering formatting characters

```
Date/Time Formats

Number  Meaning
  1     Day of the month
  2     Month (number)
  3     Month (word)
  4     Year (all four digits)
  5     Year (last two digits)
  6     Day of the week (word)
  7     Hour (24 hour clock)
  8     Hour (12 hour clock)
  9     Minute
  0     am / pm
  #     Week  (number)
  %     Pad numbers less than 10 with a leading zero, or
        Output only 3 letters for the month or day of the week
  $     Pad numbers less than 10 with a leading space

Examples: 3 1, 4  Wk # = January 15, 1991 Wk 3
          %6 %3 1, 4  = Tue Jan 15, 1991
          %2/%1/5 (6) = 01/15/91 (Tuesday)
          8:90        = 10:55am

1 Date Format; 2 Time Format; 3 Start Day of Week; 4 DOS Time; 5 DOS Date: 0
```

Figure 13.2: The Date/Time Formats screen

Date/time options

The following list describes the use of each date/time option. Press the number or highlighted letter to select an option.

- Date Format and Time Format: Type in the date and time format using the appropriate formatting numbers.

- Start Day of Week: Press ← or → to select the day upon which each week of the Calendar display will begin.

- DOS Date and DOS Time: Type in the current time and date to change your computer's clock.

After you select your date/time formats, press F7 twice to return to the Calendar.

Working with Calendar Alarms

Using an alarm

You can make appointments with an asterisk (*) when you want an alarm to alert you to the impending appointment. If you want the alarm to sound no matter what program you are

working in, you should add the CL/I command to your
AUTOEXEC.BAT file (make sure Office PC is in your path).
With the Alarms option, you can specify the number of minutes before an appointment for the alarm to sound and the
time interval between rings.

To change the alarm times, follow these instructions:

1. Press 2 or S (Setup) from the Calendar menu.

2. Press 2 or A (Alarms). The Alarm Options menu (Figure 13.3) appears and offers you two choices.

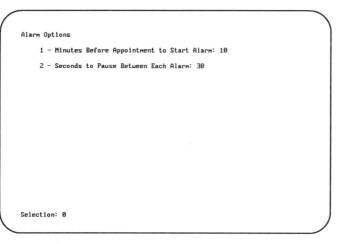

```
Alarm Options

    1 - Minutes Before Appointment to Start Alarm: 10

    2 - Seconds to Pause Between Each Alarm: 30













Selection: 0
```

Figure 13.3: The Alarm Options screen

3. Press 1 or M to change the number of minutes prior to
   the appointment time that the alarm will sound, or
   press 2 or S to change the time interval between
   alarms.

4. Press F7 twice to return to the Calendar.

Setting Appointments and To-Do List Options

You can use several options to configure the way you want the appointments and to-do items to be entered into the Appointments and To-Do List windows.

1. To select an Appointments/To-Do option, press 2 or O (Options) from the Calendar menu.

2. Then, press 3 or T (Appointments/To-Do). The Appointments/To-Do Options menu appears (Figure 13.4).

3. Select the appropriate option from the menu and make the changes you want.

4. Press F7 twice to return to the Calendar.

```
Appointments/To-Do Options

    Appointment Outline
        1 - Beginning Time: 8:00am
        2 - Ending Time: 6:00pm
        3 - Time Interval (in minutes): 60

    4 - Appointment Overlap Display: Yes

    5 - Single Line Display (Memo, Appts, To-Do): No

    6 - Auto-Alarm Mode (Appts): No

    7 - Auto-Mark mode (To-Do): No

    8 - Unique Priorities (To-Do): Yes




    Selection: 0
```

Figure 13.4: The Appointments/To-Do Options screen

*Appoint-
ments &
To-Do
options*

The following list contains a description of each Appointments/To-Do option.

*   Appointment Outline: Changes the beginning and ending times for the appointment outline, and modifies the

time interval. The default is from 8:00 a.m. until 10:00 p.m. with a 60-minute interval between appointment times.

- Appointment Overlap Display: When toggled on, displays a line in the Appointments window indicating the length of an appointment.

- Single Line Display: When toggled on, text entered in Calendar windows beyond the edge of the window will not wrap to the next line.

- Auto-Alarm Mode: When toggled on, automatically sets the alarm when you enter an appointment.

- Auto-Mark Mode: When toggled on, automatically marks each item entered on the To-Do List and automatically deletes that item at the end of the day.

- Unique Priorities: When toggled on, automatically renumbers the priority of To-Do List tasks when new tasks are inserted.

Using the Archive/Delete/Backup Option

The Archive/Delete/Backup option programs the Calendar to automatically create an archive file containing a record of old Calendar entries. Such a record is helpful when you're trying to remember an event that happened months ago. The archived file is named after the Calendar file—for example, CALENDAR.ARC.

Creating archive files

This feature will also automatically delete old Calendar entries, and you can specify the number of elapsed days before this data is deleted from the Calendar (the default is 7 days).

Archive/Delete/Backup automatically creates backup files at intervals of a specified number of minutes while you're working. Then, if a power failure occurs, you lose only those changes made since the last backup. The backup file name will have a .BK! extension.

Finally, you can use this feature to automatically save newly entered data whenever you exit to the Shell.

Selecting Calendar Colors

*Calendar
colors*

The color setup for the Calendar is the same as for the Shell. Refer to **Step 3** for a detailed discussion of setting screen colors. Colors selected for the Calendar are permanent; they will not revert to the same colors you selected for the Shell.

Changing the File Format

The File Format feature saves information created with Calendar 3.0 in the format for Calendar versions 1.1 and earlier. You can also add a password that allows you to secure your calendar file from unauthorized access.

1. Press 6 or F (File Format). Two possible file formats and the password options are displayed.

2. Select one of two formats: Calendar 1.1 and Calendar 2.0/3.0. Your Calendar data will be saved in the format you select whenever you exit from the program.

3. Options 3 (Add/Change Password) and 4 (Remove Password) allow you to enter, change, and delete a password. You will be asked to enter your password each time you start the Calendar.

Step 14 discusses the printing procedures and print options available with the Calendar.

Printing with the Calendar

The Calendar's print feature lets you print a copy of your memos, appointments, and to-do entries for a day, week, month, or year. You can also select print options that allow you to print specific categories of Calendar entries; for example, you can print memos without printing appointments or to-do entries, or only appointments and to-do entries, without printing memos, and so on. This step guides you through the procedures for printing and selecting print options.

To use the print feature, start the Shell and enter the Calendar.

Printing Calendar Entries

Printing a copy of your memos, appointments, and to-do entries is as simple as pushing two keys. Be sure to turn your printer on for this exercise.

1. Move the calendar highlight to the date containing the information you want to print.

2. Press 3 or P (Print) to display the Print menu (Figure 14.1).

3. Press 1 or P (Print) to send the job to the printer. You return to the Calendar.

The Print menu offers these options:

*   Print: Send a print job to the printer.

*   Format: Choose between a normal page printout or a merge output.

*   Options: Set page length, margins, and the number of indent spaces, as well as other advanced format

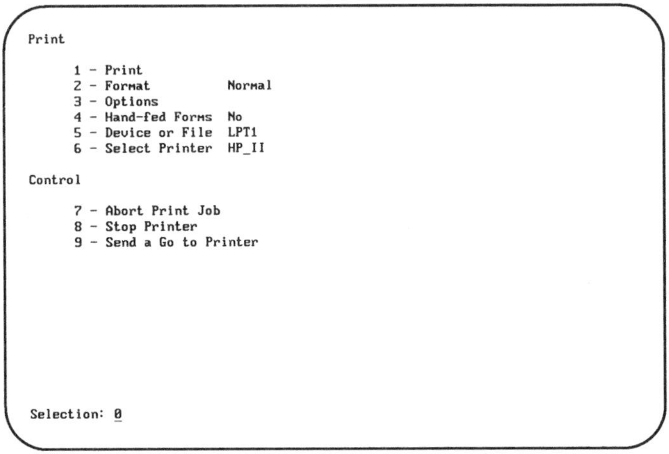

```
Print

    1 - Print
    2 - Format        Normal
    3 - Options
    4 - Hand-fed Forms  No
    5 - Device or File  LPT1
    6 - Select Printer  HP_II

Control

    7 - Abort Print Job
    8 - Stop Printer
    9 - Send a Go to Printer




Selection: 0
```

Figure 14.1: The Print menu

options. You can also select the type of calendar entries you want to print and the time period containing the entries.

- Hand-Fed Forms: Set to Yes to manually feed paper to the printer. The printer will pause and alert you to press the Send a Go to Printer command found on the Print menu.

- Device or File: Choose the printer port through which you will send a print job. This is useful when you have more than one printer. You can also elect to print to a file on the disk.

- Select Printer: Select a printer definition that matches your printer.

- Abort Print Job: Cancel the current print job.

- Stop Printer: Temporarily interrupts a print job without canceling.

- Send a Go to Printer: Restart a stopped print job or manually feed paper to the printer.

I will not cover all these options in detail, but you can easily learn to use many of them simply by experimenting.

Selecting Print Options

Let's take a look at a few commonly needed print options. This section shows you how to select the calendar entries to be printed and the time period over which these items will be printed.

1. Press 3 or P (Print) from the Calendar menu. The Print menu appears.

2. Press 3 or O (Options) to display the Print Options screen (Figure 14.2).

3. Select the options (see list below).

The following list tells you how to use each of the options on the Print Options screen.

Print options

```
  Page Size

      1 - Page Length (in lines):   66
      2 - Top Margin (in lines):     6
      3 - Bottom Margin (in lines):  6

      4 - Left Margin (column #):    10
      5 - Right Margin (column #):   74
      6 - Number of Col. to Indent:  2

  Options

      0 - One Day Per Page:  No
      E - Print Empty Days:  No
      W - WP Merge Format:   WP 5.0
      D - Duration:          Week

  Contents

      A - Appointments:  Yes
      I - To-Do Items:   Yes
      M - Memos:         Yes


  Selection: 0
```

Figure 14.2: The Print Options screen

- Page Size: Press the appropriate number or bolded letter and enter the desired page length, margins, and indent spaces.

- Options: Press the appropriate bolded letter to select the time period over which the calendar entries will be printed. The entries for a selected time period are printed forward from the date upon which the calendar highlight is resting. You can also elect to print a date heading for all days without entries.

- Contents: Press the appropriate bolded letter to toggle the Appointments, To-Do list, and Memos options on (print) or off (no print).

When you finish making selections, press F7 twice to return to the Calendar.

Defining a Printer

Printer definition files

The Calendar provides several printer definition files, one of which may match the printer you are using. If you do not find a matching printer definition, you can select a file called GENERIC.PRD, which is a general printer definition file that should work with your printer. The generic definition file will not, however, provide the setup codes for your printer, or allow boldfacing and underlining formats.

To select a printer definition file, follow these steps, starting at the Calendar screen:

1. Press 3 or P (Print) to display the Print menu.

2. Press 6 or S (Select Printer) to display the Printer Drivers screen (Figure 14.3).

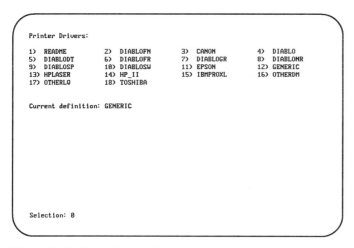

```
Printer Drivers:

  1> README        2> DIABLOFN      3> CANON        4> DIABLO
  5> DIABLODT      6> DIABLOFR      7> DIABLOGR     8> DIABLONR
  9> DIABLOSP     10> DIABLOSW     11> EPSON       12> GENERIC
 13> HPLASER      14> HP_II        15> IBMPROXL    16> OTHERDM
 17> OTHERLQ      18> TOSHIBA


Current definition: GENERIC




Selection: 0
```

Figure 14.3: The Printer Drivers screen

3. Type the number of the printer definition that matches your printer and press ↵. (If your printer is not listed, type 12 for Generic.)

4. Press F7 to return to the Calendar.

Managing Files with File Manager

File Manager may be one of the most often used Office PC programs. With File Manager, you can perform many DOS commands without ever seeing the DOS prompt. You can copy, rename, delete, and move files, and create, rename, and delete directories, and never have to type a DOS command.

This step leads you through the basic, and most often needed, file management features offered in File Manager. **Step 16** will show you how to work with directories.

Starting File Manager

Like the Office PC programs you have learned about thus far, File Manager can be started in either of two ways: from the Shell menu by pressing the assigned startup letter, or from a DOS prompt by typing FM and pressing ↵ if you are in the Office PC directory or have the Office PC directory in your path. The File Manager screen is shown in Figure 15.1.

The File Manager screen shown in Figure 15.1 displays the files for the OFFICE directory; your display may be different, depending on the directory from which you start the Shell. The File Manager screen is organized into three areas.

File Manager screen

At the top of the screen is the header information, which displays the current date and time, the directory for the file list, the amount of free RAM and disk space, the total bytes occupied by the listed files, and the number of files in the directory.

Header information

The middle of the screen displays the list of directories and files for the displayed directory. Notice that directory names,

List of directories and files

```
08-10-91  11:34a              Directory C:\OFFICE30\*.*
Free Mem: 350,592    Disk Free: 6,625,280    Used: 1,974,121         Files:  201

. <CURRENT>      <DIR>                  .. <PARENT>     <DIR>
LEARN   .        <DIR>    08-01-90  5:47p  ADDRESS .NB       3,658  06-14-90  0:12a
ALTF    .EDM     4,478    06-14-90 12:01p  ALTL    .EDM      4,956  06-14-90 12:01p
ALTM    .EDM     4,322    06-14-90 12:01p  ALTR    .EDM      5,038  06-14-90 12:01p
ALTS    .EDM     7,010    06-14-90 12:01p  ALTSHFA1.SHM      1,856  06-14-90 12:01p
ALTSHFDM.SHM     2,269    06-14-90 12:01p  ALTSHFM2.SHM      1,866  06-14-90 12:01p
ALTSHFM3.SHM     2,458    06-14-90 12:01p  ALTSHFTA.SHM      2,652  06-14-90 12:01p
ALTSHFTD.SHM     2,863    06-14-90 12:01p  ALTSHFTD.WPM     11,143  06-14-90 12:01p
ALTSHFTM.SHM     2,392    06-14-90 12:01p  ALTT    .EDM        478  06-14-90 12:01p
ALTU    .EDM       536    06-14-90 12:01p  CALC    .EXE     31,744  06-14-90  0:12a
CALC    .HLP    26,281    06-14-90  0:12a  CALC    .PIF        369  06-14-90  0:12a
CALC-W  .PIF       369    06-14-90  0:12a  CALC-W30.PIF        545  06-14-90  0:12a
CALC30  .PIF       545    06-14-90  0:12a  CANON   .PRD      1,024  06-14-90  0:12a
CHARMAP .NB     44,206    06-14-90  0:12a  CL      .EXE     84,480  06-14-90  0:12a
CL      .HLP    36,481    06-14-90  0:12a  CL      .PIF        369  06-14-90  0:12a
CL-W    .PIF       369    06-14-90  0:12a  CL-W30  .PIF        545  06-14-90  0:12a
CL30    .PIF       545    06-14-90  0:12a  CLIENT  .NB         467  06-14-90  0:12a
CL_PD   .SHM     1,609    06-14-90 12:01p  CL_PD1  .SHM      2,421  06-14-90 12:01p
CL_PDDL .PRI    17,573    06-14-90 12:01p  CL_PDDP .PRI     30,322  06-14-90 12:01p

1 *Mark; 2 Delete; 3 Move/Rename; 4 Select Files; 5 Lock; 6 Look; <F7 to Exit,
7 Other Dir; 8 Copy; 9 Word Srch; N Name Srch; F5 Find Files; 6    F3 for Help>
```

Figure 15.1: The File Manager screen

followed by <DIR>, are listed first, followed by the file names.

File Manager menu

At the bottom of the screen is the File Manager menu. You will learn how to use most of these options.

File Manager help (F3)

For a brief description of all the File Manager options, press F3 (Help). Figure 15.2 displays the Help screen. Press the assigned letter to receive help with that option. Press F3 twice to display the help template.

Locating a File Name on the List

To locate a file name on the list, press the arrow keys to move the highlight to the file name you want. You can also press F2 or N (Name Srch) and type the file name. As you type the file name, the highlight moves to a file name that matches the typed characters. When the highlight is on the file name you want, press ↵.

```
Help                              FM 3.0
  Setup: C:\OFFICE30\CLF]FM.SYS

      Press a function key to get information about the use of the key.
      Press the Help key again to see a template for the function keys.
      Press the following letters to get information about specific topics:


      A - Starting File Manager      M - Move or Rename Files
      B - The File List              N - Delete Files
      C - Copy                       O - Startup Options
      D - Directory Tree             P - Print the Directory
      E - Double Directory           Q - Program Launch
      F - Find Files                 R - Other Directories
      G - Moving the Cursor          S - Shell
      H - Name Search                T - Block Copy
      I - Select Files               U - Screen
      J - Mark Files                 V - Switch
      K - Look                       W - Word Search
      L - Lock                       Y - Customer Support Information



   A-Z Topic: 0              <Esc Topics; Space Exit; Function Key Help for Key>
```

Figure 15.2: The Help screen

Marking Files

If you want to delete, copy, move, lock, or search a group of files, use the Mark feature of File Manager.

Mark feature

1. Press the Shell startup letter to start File Manager.

2. Press the arrow cursor keys to move the highlight to the file(s) you want to mark.

3. When the highlight is on a file name, press 1 or * (Mark) to mark the file. The highlight moves to the next file, and an asterisk appears in back of the file name. Figure 15.3 shows several marked files.

4. To unmark a file name, place the highlight on the marked file name and press 1 or * (Mark).

Once the files have been marked, you can copy, delete, move, search, or lock them as a group. This feature will speed up many large file management operations.

```
08-10-91   5:39p             Directory C:\OFFICE30\*.*
Free Mem: 350,592    Disk Free: 6,619,136   Marked: 80,916        Marks: 10/202

. <CURRENT>    <DIR>                    .. <PARENT>   <DIR>
LEARN    .     <DIR>     08-01-90  5:47p  ADDRESS .NB      3,658  06-14-90  8:12a
ALTF     .EDM     4,478  06-14-90 12:01p  ALTL    .EDM     4,956  06-14-90 12:01p
ALTM     .EDM     4,322  06-14-90 12:01p  ALTR    .EDM     5,038  06-14-90 12:01p
ALTS     .EDM     7,010  06-14-90 12:01p  ALTSHFA1.SHM     1,856  06-14-90 12:01p
ALTSHFDM.SHM     2,269  06-14-90 12:01p  ALTSHFM2.SHM     1,866  06-14-90 12:01p
ALTSHFM3.SHM     2,458* 06-14-90 12:01p  ALTSHFTA.SHM     2,652* 06-14-90 12:01p
ALTSHFTD.SHM     2,863* 06-14-90 12:01p  ALTSHFTD.WPM    11,143* 06-14-90 12:01p
ALTSHFTM.SHM     2,392* 06-14-90 12:01p  ALTT    .EDM      478* 06-14-90 12:01p
ALTU     .EDM      536* 06-14-90 12:01p  CALC    .EXE    31,744* 06-14-90  8:12a
CALC     .HLP    26,281* 06-14-90  8:12a  CALC    .PIF      369* 06-14-90  8:12a
CALC-W   .PIF      369  06-14-90  8:12a  CALC-W30.PIF      545  06-14-90  8:12a
CALC30   .PIF      545  06-14-90  8:12a  CANON   .PRD     1,024  06-14-90  8:12a
CHARMAP  .NB    44,206  06-14-90  8:12a  CL      .EXE    84,480  06-14-90  8:12a
CL       .HLP    36,481  06-14-90  8:12a  CL      .PIF      369  06-14-90  8:12a
CL-W     .PIF      369  06-14-90  8:12a  CL-W30  .PIF      545  06-14-90  8:12a
CL30     .PIF      545  06-14-90  8:12a  CLIENT  .NB       467  06-14-90  8:12a
CL_PD    .SHM     1,609  06-14-90 12:01p  CL_PD1  .SHM     2,421  06-14-90 12:01p
CL_PDDL  .PRI    17,573  06-14-90 12:01p  CL_PDDP .PRI    30,322  06-14-90 12:01p

1 *Mark; 2 Delete; 3 Move/Rename; 4 Select Files; 5 Lock; 6 Look; <F7 to Exit,
7 Other Dir; 8 Copy; 9 Word Srch; N Name Srch; F5 Find Files; 6     F3 for Help>
```

Figure 15.3: Marked files

To mark all the files at one time, press Home-* or Alt-F5. Pressing Home-* or Alt-F5 also will unmark all marked files, regardless of how many files have been marked.

When working with groups of files, it is easy to lose valuable information without meaning to do so. As a safeguard, File Manager always asks if you want to perform an operation on a group of files.

Copying and Deleting Files

You can copy or delete a single file, or a group of files that have been marked with an asterisk.

1. Move the highlight to the file to be copied, or mark several files to be copied with an asterisk.

2. Press 8 or C (Copy). You are prompted for a yes or no, then the location.

3. Type the destination path (drive and directory) and press ↵. The file(s) is copied. If you try to copy over a

file with the same name, you will be asked to confirm the replacement (unless the confirmation option is turned off with the Select Files option, in which case Office PC will refuse to copy a file onto itself).

To delete a file, follow these steps:

1. Move the highlight to the file to be deleted, or mark several files to be deleted with an asterisk.

2. Press 2 or D (Delete). You are asked if you want to delete the file(s).

3. Press Y (Yes). The file name(s) disappears from the list.

Moving and Renaming a File

Moving and renaming a file are included in a single File Manager option. Although you can rename only one file at a time, you can move a group of files.

First, let's look at how to move or rename a single file.

1. Move the highlight to the file name you want to rename or move.

2. Press 3 or M (Move/Rename). The file name, including the path, is displayed at the bottom of your screen.

3. To change the name, use the arrow keys to move the cursor to the file name and make the necessary changes. To move the file, delete the old drive and/or directory name and type in the new location. You also can move the file and change the file name at the same time.

4. Press ↵. The new name replaces the old name on the list of file names, or, if you move the file, the name disappears from the current directory list.

Now, let's see how to move a group of files.

1. Mark each file to be moved with an asterisk.

2. Press 3 or M (Move/Rename).

3. Type the destination drive and/or directory (do not type a file name) and press ↵. The files are moved to the new location, and the file names disappear from the current directory list.

Securing Your Files

Many of your files may be sensitive enough to need securing from unauthorized viewing or use by other individuals. File Manager allows you to lock and unlock your files. A locked file requires a password in order to gain access to the file. As long as you do not share your password, your files will be quite secure.

To lock and unlock a file, or a group of files, you should follow these instructions:

1. Highlight the file, or mark a group of files with an asterisk.

2. Press 5 or k (Lock). You receive the following prompt: 1 Lock; 2 Unlock.

3. Press 1 or L (Lock) to lock the files, or press 2 or U (Unlock) to unlock files that have been locked. You are prompted to enter a password.

4. Type a password of up to 80 characters and press ↵. When locking a file, you are asked to type the password a second time in order to verify the correct

spelling. When unlocking a file, type the assigned password and press ↲. The files are immediately unlocked.

Viewing the Contents of a File

It can be helpful to see the information a file contains before you perform a file management operation. Use the Look feature to view a file.

1. Move the highlight to the file to be viewed.
2. Press 6 or L (Look). The contents of the file are displayed on the screen.
3. Use ↑ or ↓ to move through the document. You may also use Home-Home-↑ and Home-Home-↓ to move to the beginning and end of the document.
4. Press F7 or the spacebar to exit from the Look feature.

Other Options

The following list briefly tells you the usage of each File Manager menu item not covered so far:

*   Select Files (4): Display files according to a specified file name pattern, list files according to specified dates, specify sort parameters, change the display mode, turn the Look mode prompt on and off, and turn the file-replacement confirmation on and off.

*   Other Dir (7): Change to a different directory, designate a new default directory, or create a new directory. (For more information on Other Dir, see Step 16.)

*   Word Search (9): Search through files for a specified word or word pattern and display the file names of all the files containing such a word or word pattern.

- Find Files (5): Search for a specified file, or file name pattern, in a directory or on a disk drive.

Now that you are familiar with the file management features of File Manager, continue on with **Step 16** to see how easy it is to manage your hard-disk directories.

Managing Directories with File Manager

Working with the directory structure is another DOS function that is easily handled with File Manager. This step shows you how to create new directories, move between existing directories, delete directories that you no longer need, and create a directory tree.

Working with Directories

At the top of the file name list are two general directory indicators: . <CURRENT> <DIR> and .. <PARENT> <DIR>. The current directory is the one displayed on the screen. The parent directory is the directory to which the current directory is attached.

Changing Directories

Follow these steps to change from the current directory to the parent directory:

1. Start File Manager.
2. Move the highlight to .. <PARENT> <DIR>.
3. Press ↵. The list of files for the parent directory is displayed. (You must press ↵ twice to display the list of files if you have changed the Directory Look Method to Prompt. The Directory Look Method option is reached through the Select Files option, and the default setting is No Prompt.)

To display a file list for a directory attached to the current directory, follow these steps:

1. Place the highlight on the directory name (remember, a directory name is followed by <DIR>).

2. Press ⏎ to display the file list.

Changing the Default Directory

The default directory is the directory that is initially displayed at the top of the screen when you start File Manager. To make another directory the default directory, use the Other Dir (7) option on the File Manager menu. Here's how it works.

1. Press 7 or O (Other Dir). The current directory name is displayed.

2. Type the full path for the new default directory and press ⏎ twice. The file names for the new directory are displayed.

Creating a New Directory

When you initially select the Other Dir option, a full path is displayed on the bottom of your screen. You are then free to edit the displayed path or type in a new path. You can also type in an entirely new directory name, thereby creating a new directory.

1. Press 7 or O (Other Dir). The full path for the current directory is displayed.

2. Type a new path with a new directory name and press ⏎. You are asked if you want to create a new directory.

3. Press Y (Yes). The new directory is created.

Deleting a Directory

Before you can delete a directory from the list, you must delete or move all the files in that directory. If the directory is not empty, you will be shown an error message alerting you to this fact. Here's how it is done.

1. Move the highlight to the directory you want to delete and press ↵ to display the file names.

2. Move or delete the files in the directory.

3. Move the highlight to .. <PARENT> <DIR> and press ↵ to return to the parent directory.

4. Once again, place the highlight on the directory you want to delete.

5. Press 2 or D (Delete). The directory disappears from the file list.

Using the Screen Feature

The Screen feature allows you to display your directories and file lists in various forms. You can display two different file lists at the same time, display a graphic representation (directory tree) of all your directories, display a directory tree and a file list on your screen at the same time, and so on.

Screen feature

We won't be able to do an exercise for all the display variations available with the Screen feature, but the following exercises will get you up and running quickly.

Displaying Two File Lists with Half Screen and Full Screen

The Half Screen option lets you display two different file lists on your screen at the same time. The Full Screen option lets you display two directories, each directory occupying a full screen. Let's try both options.

1. Start File Manager.

2. Press Ctrl-F3 to display the Screen options, as shown in Figure 16.1.

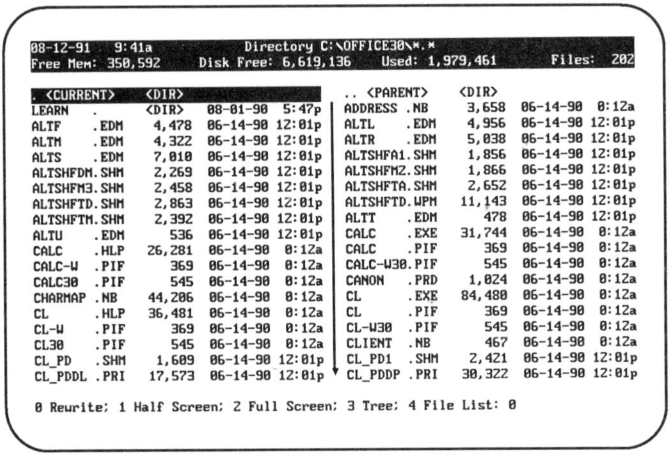

```
08-12-91    9:41a           Directory C:\OFFICE30\*.*
Free Mem: 350,592    Disk Free: 6,619,136    Used: 1,979,461        Files: 202

. <CURRENT>   <DIR>                  .. <PARENT>   <DIR>
LEARN    .       <DIR>    08-01-90   5:47p   ADDRESS .NB      3,658   06-14-90   8:12a
ALTF     .EDM     4,478   06-14-90  12:01p   ALTL     .EDM    4,956   06-14-90  12:01p
ALTM     .EDM     4,322   06-14-90  12:01p   ALTR     .EDM    5,038   06-14-90  12:01p
ALTS     .EDM     7,010   06-14-90  12:01p   ALTSHFA1.SHM     1,856   06-14-90  12:01p
ALTSHFDM.SHM      2,269   06-14-90  12:01p   ALTSHFM2.SHM     1,866   06-14-90  12:01p
ALTSHFM3.SHM      2,458   06-14-90  12:01p   ALTSHFTA.SHM     2,652   06-14-90  12:01p
ALTSHFTD.SHM      2,863   06-14-90  12:01p   ALTSHFTD.WPM    11,143   06-14-90  12:01p
ALTSHFTM.SHM      2,392   06-14-90  12:01p   ALTT     .EDM      478   06-14-90  12:01p
ALTU     .EDM       536   06-14-90  12:01p   CALC     .EXE   31,744   06-14-90   8:12a
CALC     .HLP    26,281   06-14-90   8:12a   CALC     .PIF      369   06-14-90   8:12a
CALC-W   .PIF       369   06-14-90   8:12a   CALC-W30.PIF       545   06-14-90   8:12a
CALC30   .PIF       545   06-14-90   8:12a   CANON    .PRD    1,024   06-14-90   8:12a
CHARMAP  .NB     44,286   06-14-90   8:12a   CL       .EXE   84,480   06-14-90   8:12a
CL       .HLP    36,481   06-14-90   8:12a   CL       .PIF      369   06-14-90   8:12a
CL-W     .PIF       369   06-14-90   8:12a   CL-W30   .PIF      545   06-14-90   8:12a
CL30     .PIF       545   06-14-90   8:12a   CLIENT   .NB       467   06-14-90   8:12a
CL_PD    .SHM     1,609   06-14-90  12:01p   CL_PD1   .SHM    2,421   06-14-90  12:01p
CL_PDDL  .PRI    17,573   06-14-90  12:01p ▼ CL_PDDP  .PRI   30,322   06-14-90  12:01p

0 Rewrite; 1 Half Screen; 2 Full Screen; 3 Tree; 4 File List: 0
```

Figure 16.1: The Screen options

*Screen
options*

The Screen options can be summarized as follows:

Rewrite   Allows you to manually rewrite, or update, the screen display.

Half Screen   Displays two directories on the same screen—one on the left side, the other on the right.

Full Screen   Displays two directories using the entire screen; press Shift-F3 or Tab to switch from the first directory to the second.

Tree   Displays the directory structure in a tree format.

File List   Changes a directory tree into a file list.

*Half
Screen*

3. Press 1 or H (Half Screen). The file list is displayed on the left side of the screen. Notice the arrows pointing to the left on the center divider.

4. Press Shift-F3 or Tab to designate a second directory for viewing. You are prompted to type in the directory name.

5. Type the directory name and press ↵. The second directory appears on the right side of your screen.

6. Press Shift-F3 or Tab to move between the two directories.

7. Press Ctrl-F3, 2 or S (Full Screen) to display a single file list on the full screen.

    Full Screen

8. Press Shift-F3 or Tab to switch between the two directories, each occupying a full screen when displayed.

Displaying a Directory Tree

A directory tree is helpful for viewing all your directories on a single screen.

1. Press Ctrl-F3 (Screen) to display the Screen options.

2. Press 3 or T (Tree). You are prompted to type the name of the directory where you want the highlight to appear on the tree.

3. Type the directory name and press ↵. The directory structure appears on the left side of the screen.

4. Press the ↑ or ↓ key to move the highlight to any directory where you want to view a list of files, and press ↵.

You *must* press ↵ to select the directory, or you will not be able to display the file list for that directory.

5. Press Shift-F3 or Tab. The file list for that directory appears on your screen.

6. Press Shift-F3 or Tab to return to the directory tree. You can now select a second directory for viewing.

7. To disable the Directory Tree mode, be sure the tree is displayed and press Ctrl-F3, 4 or F (File List), and press ⌐ (you can type in the name of a new directory prior to pressing ⌐).

The above examples are only a sample of the various combinations of directories and tree displays you can have. With a little experimentation, you'll soon discover you can display such things as a directory tree on one side of your screen and a file list on the other, or a directory tree on the left and another tree on the right, and so on. Your preferred display can be saved in setup (Shift-F1, 3).

Using the Clipboard with File Manager

The Clipboard is used to transfer the contents of a file into the Clipboard buffer, and from the Clipboard buffer into a shell-compatible program.

The Clipboard is not available from the DOS prompt. The following procedure works only if you are in the Shell.

To transfer text using the Clipboard, move the highlight to the file name, press Ctrl-F1, and select Save or Append. The contents of the file are stored in the Clipboard buffer. You can exit from the File Manager and start any shell-compatible program from the Office PC main menu. Place the cursor where you want the contents of the Clipboard buffer to appear, and press Ctrl-F1 and R to retrieve the data onto your screen.

Organizing Your Desktop with the Notebook

The Office PC Notebook is an excellent desktop organizer, helping you keep track of names, addresses, telephone numbers, and important information about your many friends, business associates, and clients. This step is merely a basic introduction to the organizational powers of the Notebook, designed to get you up and running as soon as possible. With some experimentation, you will be able to take advantage of all the capabilities of the Notebook.

Starting the Notebook

You can start the Notebook in two ways: by pressing the startup letter on the Shell menu, or from DOS by typing **NB** at the DOS prompt if Office PC is in your path or you are in the Office PC directory.

Starting the Note- book

The initial screen for the Notebook is blank (Figure 17.1). This screen is called the *List Display*. The List Display is an index of the entries recorded in the Notebook. This index often comprises names and phone numbers, but can be customized to contain other information.

List Display screen

An entry does not appear on the List Display until you create a *record* for that entry. A record is similar to an index card that contains information about an individual. Each piece of information entered in a record is called a *field*. For example, a name, phone number, and address are three separate fields.

Records

Fields

When you create your first notebook file and save it, you are prompted to name the file NOTEBOOK.NB. The Notebook will automatically retrieve the file named NOTEBOOK.NB when you start the program. You can create several notebook

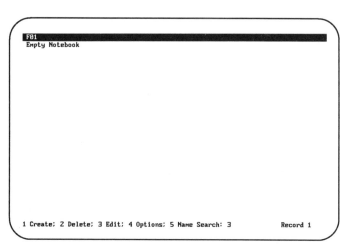

Figure 17.1: The initial List Display

files and save them with different names. In **Step 19**, you'll learn how to create a new notebook file. The next section of this step shows you how to retrieve an existing notebook file.

F3 (Help)

As with the other Office PC programs you have worked with, pressing F3 displays a help screen that lists several categories containing helpful information about how to use the Notebook features. Figure 17.2 shows you the basic help screen. Press the letter preceding the item you want help with. Press F3 twice to display the help template.

The files that are needed to run the Notebook are called NB.EXE (program file), NOTEBOOK.NEW (system file), and NOTEBOOK.HLP (help file).

Retrieving a Notebook File

The Notebook comes with five sample notebook files called ADDRESS.NB, EMPLOYEE.NB, CONTACT.NB, INVENTOR.NB, and PROJECT.NB. Instead of creating a

```
  Help                                    NB 3.0
        Setup file:

        Press any function key to get information about the use of the key.
        Press Help <F3> again to see a template for the function keys.
        Press the following letters to get information about specific topics:

        A - Startup Options                 I - Setup
        B - List Display                    J - Options for Current Notebook
        C - Record Display
        D - Adding & Deleting Records
        E - Printing
        F - Dialing
        G - Merging a Notebook File         Y - Customer Support Information
        H - Search                          Z - Character Set- Compose




  A-Z Topic:                <ESC Topics; Space Exit; Function Key Help for Key>
```

Figure 17.2: The Notebook help screen

List Display from scratch, we will retrieve the ADDRESS.NB
file and demonstrate how to use the Notebook.

1. Press Shift-F10 (Retrieve).

2. Type **ADDRESS** and press ↵. The ADDRESS.NB List
   Display appears on your screen (Figure 17.3).

Each entry on the list represents a single record. The first and
last name, work phone, home phone, and company represent
five fields from each record.

Editing a Notebook Record

A notebook record is composed of *labels* and *fields,* which
are separated by lines. A label identifies the information you
enter in a field. Let's take a look at how you modify a label
and edit a field from the ADDRESS.NB file. Be sure that the
ADDRESS.NB List Display is on your screen.

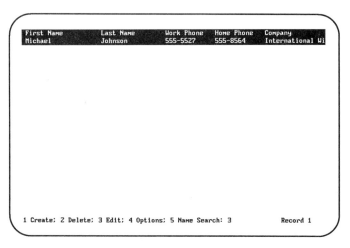

First Name	Last Name	Work Phone	Home Phone	Company
Michael	Johnson	555-5527	555-8564	International Wi

1 Create; 2 Delete; 3 Edit; 4 Options; 5 Name Search: 3   Record 1

Figure 17.3: The ADDRESS.NB sample List Display

1. To display a record, use the cursor keys to move the highlight to an entry on the List Display and press ↵. See Figure 17.4 for an example record.

2. Press Tab to move forward through the fields. Press Shift-Tab to move backward.

3. Use the standard WordPerfect editing keys to edit the data in a field (Delete, Backspace, Insert, and cursor keys).

4. Press F7 to return to the List Display.

5. To edit a record label, field size and position, and the box borders, press Shift-F8 to display the Options for Current Notebook menu line.

6. Press 2 or R (Record display) to place the record in the format mode (Figure 17.5).

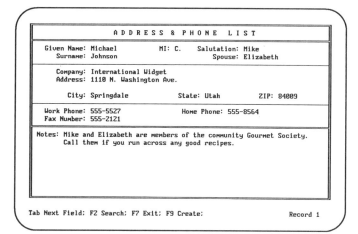

Figure 17.4: Sample record

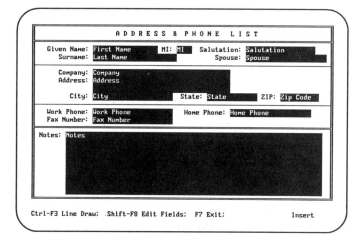

Figure 17.5: The record format screen

In the figure, fields are shown in reverse video. Text displayed inside the fields are the *field names*. Text displayed outside the fields are *labels*. The menu at the bottom of the screen provides options for editing the fields and box borders.

7. Use the arrow keys to move the cursor to the label to be edited.

8. Press Insert to change to typeover mode.

Editing with Insert turned on will move the box lines, necessitating repair work on the boxes.

9. Type the new label. Pressing the spacebar will delete text at the cursor position.

10. To edit a field, press Shift-F8. The editing options are displayed on the bottom of your screen. You can change the size, position, and name of a field, and create a new field or delete an obsolete field.

11. Press Tab and Shift-Tab to move between fields. Use the cursor keys to resize and/or reposition a field. Experiment with each of these options to see how they work. Within minutes, you will understand how to modify your own records to suit your needs.

12. Press F7 three times to return to the List Display screen.

Adding a Record to the List Display

You can add a new record to the List Display directly from the List Display screen.

1. From the List Display screen, press Shift-F10, type **address**, then press ↵. The currently selected record is displayed.

2. Press F9 (Add rec). A blank record appears.

3. Press Tab to move between fields, and type in the appropriate information.

4. Press F7 to return to the List Display. The new record appears on the list.

Deleting a Record from the List Display

You can quickly and easily delete an obsolete record directly from the List Display.

1. Move the highlight to the record to be deleted.

2. Press the Delete key. You are asked if you want to delete the record from the list.

3. Press Y, and the record disappears. The records below the deleted record adjust upward to fill in the empty slot. If you change your mind, press N or ↲ and the record will not be deleted.

Using the Clipboard with the Notebook

You can use the Clipboard to transfer information recorded in a record into other shell-compatible programs, or to another notebook record. This is a handy way to transfer a record into another notebook file, saving you from having to create the same record from scratch. If you haven't created your own notebook file, retrieve the ADDRESS.NB notebook file to the screen for this exercise.

*Transfer-
ring text*

1. Move the highlight to the record you want to copy into the Clipboard buffer. If you want to copy more than one record, type an asterisk (*) in front of each record.

2. Press Ctrl-F1 to display the Clipboard options.

3. Press 2 or S (Save) to save the contents of the record(s) to the buffer, or press 3 or A (Append) to append the information to data already stored in the buffer.

*Moving
between
fields*

Follow these instructions to move information in one field to another field.

1. Select a record from the List Display, and press ↵.

2. Press Tab to move the cursor to the field you want to transfer into the Clipboard buffer.

3. Press Ctrl-F1 and select Save or Append.

You can retrieve the data into a different field in the same record, or into a field in a new record (press F9 to display an empty record). You can also return to the List Display, select an existing record, and retrieve the text into a field in that record. You can exit to the Office PC main menu and start another shell-compatible program, such as WordPerfect, and retrieve the data into a document.

4. After you place the cursor where you want the text to appear, press Ctrl-F1 and select Retrieve. The Clipboard data is inserted in the new location.

Selecting Notebook Colors

You can customize the Notebook colors to enhance the appearance of the screen. If you have read **Step 5**, you are familiar with the procedures for selecting colors, so the description here will be brief.

*Choosing
colors*

To choose new colors, press Shift-F1 from the List Display screen. Then, press 3 or D (Display). Choose the type of monitor and text display you want to use, and then select your colors. These colors will always be in effect when you start the Notebook.

Exiting from the Notebook

When exiting from the Notebook, you are asked if you want to save the current notebook displayed on your screen. If you have made changes to the Notebook, you will definitely want to save the edited version. If you are familiar with Word-Perfect, the exit procedures are exactly the same. Let's try it.

Exit (F7)

1. Press F7. You are asked if you want to save the file.

2. Press Y or ↲ if you want to save, or press N if you do not want to save (you are asked if you want to exit from the Notebook; if you want to exit, press Y).

3. If you are saving, the file name is displayed. You can edit the current file name, or press ↲ to accept the current file name. If you accept the current file name, you are asked if you want to replace the old version of the Notebook.

4. Press Y to overwrite the old version with the new version. You are asked if you want to exit.

5. Press Y. You return to the Shell menu.

If you want to cancel the exit procedure at any point, press F1 (Cancel). If you want to save a notebook file without exiting, press F10 and follow the prompts.

In **Step 18,** you'll learn how to sort and print the List Display and how to print a record.

Sorting & Printing with the Notebook

15

This step teaches you how to use the Notebook's sorting feature to keep the List Display organized. You will also learn how to print a copy of the List Display and Notebook records.

Sorting the List Display

Much of the work you do with the Notebook takes place at the List Display. Here you find a display of the most important information you use from each record. For example, in the CONTACT.NB notebook file, the information you'd refer to most often are names and phone numbers.

The Notebook provides a sorting feature that keeps the entries in the List Display organized. As you update the List Display, the entries in the leftmost column are sorted in alphabetical order. In the CONTACT.NB display, the leftmost column contains names. These names are arranged alphabetically by first names, because the first name is recorded first in the name field in each record.

Sorting feature

The List Display is automatically sorted whenever you make an appropriate change to the List Display or to a record. You can disable the automatic sort procedure if you want to edit several records before sorting takes place; to use manual sorting, press Ctrl-F9. If you retain automatic sorting, the list will be sorted after you edit each record. Let's look at how you turn automatic sorting on and off.

Auto-matic sorting

1. Start the Notebook and retrieve the CONTACT.NB file.

2. Press 4 or O (Options) to display the Options for Current Notebook screen, shown in Figure 18.1.

3. Press 3 or A (Auto-Sort). To turn autosort off, press N (No). To turn autosort on, press Y (Yes).

4. Press F7 to return to the List Display.

5. To sort the entire file when autosort is disabled, press Ctrl-F9, Y.

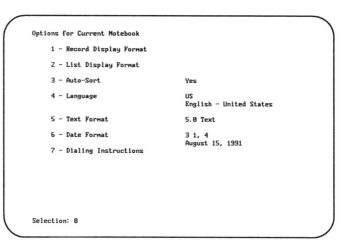

```
Options for Current Notebook

     1 - Record Display Format

     2 - List Display Format

     3 - Auto-Sort                      Yes

     4 - Language                       US
                                        English - United States

     5 - Text Format                    5.0 Text

     6 - Date Format                    3 1, 4
                                        August 15, 1991
     7 - Dialing Instructions




     Selection: 0
```

Figure 18.1: Options for Current Notebook screen

If you use European characters in your documents, option 4 on the Options for Current Notebook menu lets you select from 21 languages for sorting.

Printing the List Display

Printing

It is always a good idea to have a hard copy of any document as a backup in case of loss or damage to your storage disks. Therefore, the Notebook allows you to print a copy of the List Display. If you want, you can also print a group of selected records without printing the entire list. You do this by marking the individual records with an asterisk. Let's look at how you print the entire CONTACT.NB List Display and selected records.

1. To print the entire list display, press Shift-F7. To print selected records, place an asterisk in front of each entry you want to print, then press Shift-F7 from the List Display screen. In both instances, the Print options are displayed, as shown in Figure 18.2.

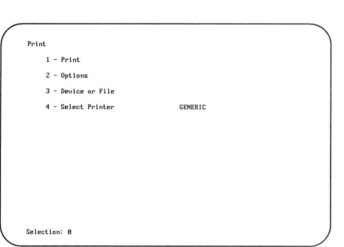

```
Print

     1 - Print

     2 - Options

     3 - Device or File

     4 - Select Printer          GENERIC




Selection: 0
```

Figure 18.2: The Print options

2. Press 2 or O (Options) for page formatting options.

3. Press 3 or D (Device or File) to change the port your printer is connected to. This is useful when you have more than one printer. You can also print to a file.

4. Press 4 or S (Select Printer) to select the exact printer you are using. The default printer is called GENERIC, which you should use if your printer does not appear on the list. (For a more complete discussion of the Definition print option, refer to **Step 14**.)

5. Press 1 or P (Print) to print the List Display or selected records.

Printing a Record

You can also print all the information contained in a record—including information that does not appear on the List Display. The following instructions guide you through the procedure for printing a record.

1. Place the highlight on the record you want to print and press ↵. The record is displayed.

2. Press Shift-F7 to display the print options.

3. Press 1 or P (Print). The record prints.

Step 19 provides the basic instructions you'll need to construct your own notebook records.

Creating a New Notebook File

If you have read **Steps 17** and **18,** you have a good idea of how the Notebook is laid out. You can edit the ADDRESS.NB notebook file to suit your purposes, but you can also design and create your own version of a notebook file. Once you experiment with the options available for building a notebook file, you'll see how easy it is.

Remember that each item of information recorded in a notebook record is called a field. So, before you start, it is helpful to determine the number, approximate size, and name of each field. It can be helpful if you draw a rough design of the record on a separate sheet of paper.

Specifying each field

There are four steps to creating a notebook record: drawing the lines, entering labels, placing fields, and creating the List Display. The following exercises guide you through these procedures.

Creating a record

Using Line Draw

After you've done your initial record planning and made a sketch of the prospective record, start the Notebook with a clear screen. If there is a List Display showing on your monitor, press F7, N, N to clear the screen.

1.   Press 4 or O (Options). The Options for Current Notebook menu appears.

2.   Press 1 or R (Record Display Format). The Record Display options appear, as shown in Figure 19.1. This is where you will create your record.

3.   Press Shift-F8 (Edit Fields).

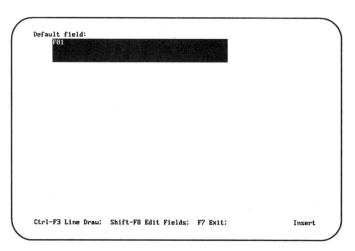

Figure 19.1: The Record Display Format options

4. Press ⏎ until the default field F01 is at the bottom of the screen. This gives you a clear area in which to place the record lines.

5. Press the arrow keys to move the cursor to the location where you want to begin drawing the field boxes.

Line Draw
(Ctrl-F3)

6. Press Ctrl-F3 (Line Draw). The Line Draw options appear.

7. Press 1, 2, or 3 to draw lines with the selected symbol. Press 4 (Change) to choose between eight other line thicknesses, or select your own symbol. Press 5 or E (Erase) to erase existing lines. Press 6 or M (Move) to move the cursor without entering new lines or displacing other screen entries.

8. When you have finished constructing the record outline, press F7, F1, or ⏎ to turn off Line Draw and return to the Record Display Format options.

Take some time to experiment with each of these options. If at any time you want to cancel what you've created and

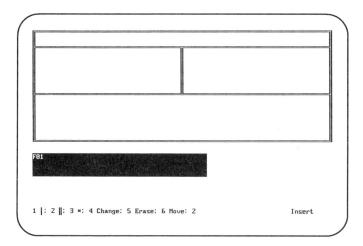

Figure 19.2: A sample record structure

start over, press F7 twice to return to the List Display, then press F7, N, N to clear the display. Figure 19.2 is an example of what a record structure might look like.

Entering a Label in a Record

After you create a record box with Line Draw, you can enter a label that identifies the type of information that will be entered in the field assigned to that box. These labels appear on the record display. The record boxes created in the preceding exercise should be on the screen with the Record Display Format options on the bottom of the screen.

1. Press Insert to change to Typeover mode. (*Typeover* appears in the lower right corner of your screen.)

2. Use the arrow keys to position the cursor in the field where you want to enter the label.

3. Type the label.

Figure 19.3 shows an example of the kinds of labels you can place on a record.

In Typeover mode, you can use the spacebar to delete characters by typing over them. You can also use the Backspace key to delete characters.

```
                    PERSONAL PHONE LIST

 NAME                                    ADDRESS



 PERSONAL INFORMATION




 F01



 Ctrl-F3 Line Draw:  Shift-F8 Edit Fields:  F7 Exit:        RECORD 1
```

Figure 19.3: Sample record labels

Do not use the Delete key to delete characters. Doing so will pull to the left the line sections located to the right of the cursor and any text located on the cursor line. This can cause confusion and require some creative repair work.

Working with Fields

In this section, you will learn how to enter a field name, position a field into a record box, change the size of a field, and add and delete a field. When you've completed these procedures, you will be on your way to creating your own notebook files.

Entering a Field Name

Now that you have created the record structure, it is time to enter the field name into the field.

1. From the Record Display options, press Shift-F8 (Edit Fields). The cursor moves into the first field (F01), and the Edit Field options appear.

2. Press 3 or N (Name).

3. Type the name of the field. A field name identifies the information that will be entered in the field. For example, if the field will contain a person's name, type **NAME**.

4. Press ↵. The F01 is replaced with the field name, as shown in Figure 19.4.

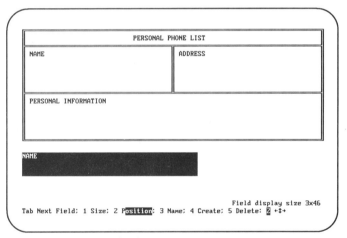

Figure 19.4: Sample field name

Positioning a Field on a Record

A field can be placed anywhere on a record, but you will want to place it in the appropriate box you created with Line Draw.

1. Press 2 or P (Position) from the Edit Field options.

2. Use the arrow keys to position the field into the box you want.

Sizing a Field

After you position a field in its box, you can make it smaller or larger, adjusting its size until it fits correctly in the box.

1. Press 1 or S (Size) from the Edit Field options.

2. Use the arrow keys to adjust the size of the field to the box borders.

Adding a New Field

So far, you have worked with a single field. You will, of course, have more than one field and will want to create additional fields. Adding a field to the record display is simple.

1. With the Edit Fields options on your screen, press 4 or C (Create) to display a second field (F02). You are prompted to enter a field name, as shown in Figure 19.5.

2. Type the field name and press ⤶. You can now position and size the new field in the appropriate location.

Deleting a Field

If you decide at some point that you no longer need a field, you can easily delete it from the record. Here's how you do it.

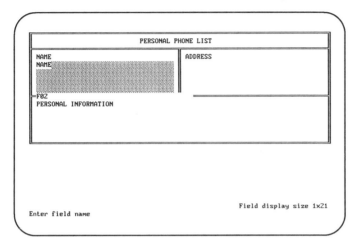

```
                    PERSONAL PHONE LIST
 NAME                            ADDRESS
 NAME
 F02
 PERSONAL INFORMATION



                                    Field display size 1x21
 Enter field name
```

Figure 19.5: Entering a field name

The Edit Fields option should be displayed on the bottom of your screen.

1. Press Tab to move the cursor to the field you want to delete.

2. Press 5 or D (Delete). You are asked if you want to delete the field, and warned that this field will be deleted from every record you have created in this notebook file.

3. Press Y (Yes) to delete the field. It disappears from the record display.

4. Press F7 three times to return to the List Display.

Creating the List Display

After you create your records and enter the personal information into each field, you can place titles and records on the List Display.

You create a List Display title by placing the name of a field from the record display at the top of the List Display screen. After these titles are in place, the appropriate information from each record is automatically displayed under the correct title.

For this exercise, be sure the List Display is on your screen. You already see the name of the first field in a record at the top of your screen. You will learn how to change the size of the title field, add a new title field, select the title name, and delete an obsolete title.

1. Press 4 or O (Options) to display the Options for Current Notebook menu.

2. Press 2 or L (List Display Format) to display the List Display Format options.

3. Press 1 or L (List Display). The name of the first field appears.

4. Press the ← and → keys to change the size of the field. Be sure to include enough space for the field information to appear on the List Display.

5. Press the Insert key to add a new title field to the display. The new field has the same name as the first field.

6. Press Tab twice to move the cursor to the new title field.

7. Press the ↑ or ↓ key to cycle through all the record field names.

8. Select the field name you want to appear as a title at the top of the List Display and size it.

9. Repeat steps 5 and 6 until you have selected and sized the most important title fields you want to appear on your List Display.

10. To delete a title field, press Tab or Shift-Tab to move to the field to be deleted and press the Delete key. You are asked if you want to delete the field.

    Moving between fields

11. Press Y (Yes). The field disappears from the screen.

12. Press F7. You are asked if you want to sort the list.

13. Press Y (Yes).

14. Press F7 twice to return to the List Display. The appropriate information from each record will be automatically placed under the corresponding title.

Refer to **Step 17** for additional information about adding, deleting, and editing records listed on the List Display.

Step 20 gives you a brief introduction on how to set up your modem and dial a phone number with the Notebook.

Using Your Modem with the Notebook

In addition to storing telephone numbers in notebook records, you can use the Notebook to dial the numbers through your modem. The Notebook works best with a Hayes-compatible modem, but you can still use it if your modem is noncompatible. This step shows you how to set up the Notebook to work with your modem and how to dial telephone numbers.

This feature is used strictly for dialing. It is not for communicating with other computers or bulletin boards.

Setting Up Your Modem

By default, the Notebook is set up to work with a Hayes-compatible modem using COM1 and the initialization and termination strings for a touch-tone modem using the AT command set. If your modem is noncompatible, you will need to know the correct initialization string and termination string for your modem. Your modem documentation will have this information. Also, you will need to know which port (COM1, COM2, COM3, or COM4) your modem is connected to. The Notebook communicates with the modem at a baud rate of 300, 8 data bits, 2 stop bits, and no parity. Let's take a look at the modem setup procedure for the Notebook.

1. From the List Display, press Shift-F1 (Setup).

2. Press 4 or M (Modem). The Modem Setup screen appears (Figure 20.1).

3. If you need to change the COM port, press 1 or C (COM Device) and type 1 for COM1, 2 for COM2, 3 for COM3, or 4 for COM4.

4. If your modem is not Hayes-compatible, press 2 or I (Initialization String), 3 or E (Edit), and type in the

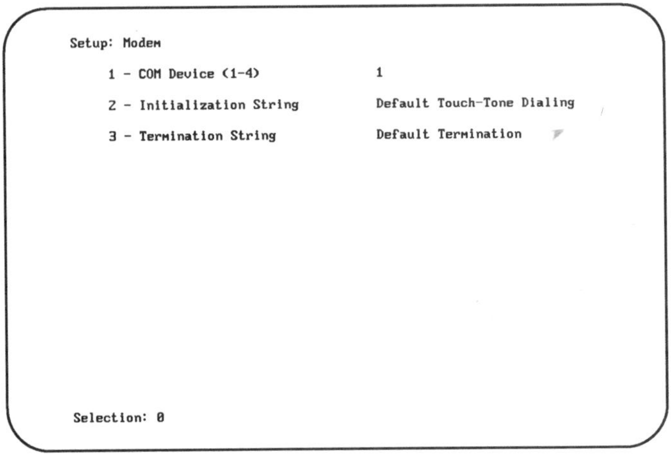

```
Setup: Modem

    1 - COM Device (1-4)              1

    2 - Initialization String         Default Touch-Tone Dialing

    3 - Termination String            Default Termination


    Selection: 0
```

Figure 20.1: The Modem Setup screen

correct string for your modem. Then, press F7 to exit. To tell the Notebook if your phone has touch-tone or pulse (rotary) dialing, press 2 or I. Then press 1 or T (Touch-Tone Dialing) or 2 or P (Pulse Dialing).

5. If your modem is not Hayes-compatible, press 3 or E (Termination String) and type in the correct string for your modem. Then, press F7 to exit.

The modem setup is now defined for the Notebook, and you are ready to begin dialing numbers.

Assigning Dialing Instructions

Phone fields

After you have set up your modem to work with the Notebook, you must assign dialing instructions for each *phone field* in your notebook file. A phone field is any field that contains a telephone number. In this exercise, you will learn how to assign program-wide instructions to a phone field. These program-wide instructions not only affect the phone field to which they are assigned, but they also pertain to that same phone field in every record of the notebook file.

Retrieve the ADDRESS.NB sample notebook file to your screen for this exercise. (You can, of course, use any notebook file.)

1. From the List Display, press 4 or O (Options).

2. Press 7 or D (Dialing Instructions). The Dialing Instructions screen appears (Figure 20.2). The first field name with existing dialing instructions is highlighted (Work Phone, in this example).

```
Options: Dialing Instructions

        Field Name                      Dialing Instruction
     ┌ Work Phone                        @
     ↑ Home Phone                        @
     │ Fax Number                        @
     │ Notes                             [None]


        Special Dialing Characters
     @   = Dial using the field contents    ?   = Prompt the user for instructions
     A-Z = Replace with a dialing sequence   0-9 = Dial the selected digit
                                              ,   = Pause two seconds
        Dialing Sequences
     A - ?                 J -                      S -
     B -                   K -                      T -
     C -                   L - 1                    U -
     D -                   M -                      V -
     E -                   N -                      W -
     F -                   O - 9                    X -
     G -                   P -                      Y -
     H -                   Q -                      Z -
     I -                   R -

     ↕ Prev/Next Field; Tab Edit Dialing Instruction; A-Z Edit Sequence: @ (F3 Help)
```

Figure 20.2: The Dialing Instructions screen

3. Press the ↑ or ↓ key to move the highlight to each of the field names.

Notice the @ symbol next to each phone number under the Dialing Instruction column. The @ symbol tells the Notebook to dial the number recorded in this phone field for every record in the notebook file. In the ADDRESS.NB file, the @ symbol has already been assigned to the phone fields.

4. To enter the @ symbol, press Tab to move the cursor to the Dialing Instruction column and type the @ symbol.

5. Press F7 to return to the List Display. You can now begin dialing numbers.

6. Follow steps 3 and 4 above to assign the @ dialing instruction to any additional phone fields.

7. When you have finished assigning dialing instructions to the phone fields, press F7 to return to the List Display.

Assigning dialing sequences

The lower portion of the Dialing Instructions screen is used to assign specific dialing sequences to records. This procedure is beyond the scope of this book, but a brief description may satisfy your curiosity. You use sequences to create a shortcut method of assigning dialing instructions to phone fields.

For example, if you have a Notebook file where all the phone numbers have the same long-distance area code and you need to dial **8** to get an outside line from your work phone, you can assign the number **8** to the letter A, the long-distance prefix **1** to the letter B, and the area code to the letter C. Then, when you assign the dialing instructions for the phone field, you simply type **ABC@**, where @ is the local phone number. Thus, you do not have to type the 8-1-(area code) portion of the phone number in each record in the Notebook file.

When you tell the Notebook to dial the number in the phone field, it will dial 8 (sequence A), 1 (sequence B), the area code (sequence C), and finally the phone number (@).

Dialing Telephone Numbers

Now that you know how to set up your modem and assign dialing instructions, you need to know how to tell the Notebook to dial a phone number.

1. Turn on your modem.

2. From the List Display, move the highlight to the record for which you want to dial a number.

3. Press F4 (Dial). If you have only one phone field for the record, the number will be dialed. If you have more than one number, you will be asked to select the number you want by pressing Tab.

4. Press Tab to place the highlight on the number and press ↵. The number is dialed.

Index

A

active programs, 10
alarms, 62, 69, 80–81
Alt menu, 32
angle in degrees, 54
annuities, 47–49
Append option, in Clip-
    board, 30
Appointment
    Calendar, 61–65. *See also*
    Calendar
appointments, 69–73
    editing and deleting, 72
    entering, 70–71
    restoring deleted, 72–73
    setting options for,
    82–83
Appointments window, 61,
    62
Archive/Delete/Backup
    option, 83
asterisk (*)
    for active programs, 10
    for alarms, 80–81
AT command set, 129
Auto-Alarm mode, 83
AUTOEXEC.BAT file
    CL/I command in, 81
    directory path in, 17
    modifying, 3
    for starting Office PC
    Shell, 5–8
Auto-Mark mode, 83
automatic sorting, 115–116
average, calculating, 57

B

background colors, 24
backup files, automatic
    creation of, 83–84
Basic Installation option, 2
BIN numerical display, 32
blocks of text, copying, 29

C

C:> prompt, 1
Calculator, 31–37
    Display Register in, 33
    financial functions on,
    45–50
    grand totals from, 36–37
    Help for, 34
    Key Function box for, 45,
    55
    Memory Register for, 36
    numerical display in, 32

programmer functions in, 57–60
Scientific, 51–54
screen colors for, 37
starting, 31–32
statistical functions in, 55–57
transferring text from, 27
Calculator tape, 33, 39–43
erasing, 39
Look option for, 41–43
printing contents of, 40
saving as file, 41
turning off and on, 39
Calendar, 61–65
archive files for, 83
Clipboard with, 64–65
Date option in, 77–78
editing function keys in, 67–68
file format for, 84
Help for, 62–63, 68
menu bar for, 62
moving through, 63–64
organizing with, 67–76
printing with, 85–89
screen colors for, 84
Setup options for, 78–84
starting, 61–63
transferring text from, 27
caret (^), 45
CL/I command, in AUTOEXEC.Bat file, 81
Clear All key (Shift-F1), 35

Clear Entry key (F1), 35
Clipboard, 27–30
with Calculator tape, 41
with Calendar, 64–65
with Display Register, 35–36
with File Manager, 104
with Notebook, 111–112
clock
12-hour, 71
24-hour, 71
resetting in computer, 79
colors. *See* screen colors
common antilog, 53
common log, 53
compound interest, 49
compressed format, 1
computer clock, resetting, 79
CONFIG.SYS file, modifying, 3
cosine, 54
counting entries, with Calculator, 56
current directory, 99
cursor movement, in Calendar, 63–64

D

DataPerfect, 27
Date Difference feature, 77, 78
date format, 15, 25–26, 79–80

Date option, in Calendar,
77–78
DEC numerical display, 32
default directory, changing,
100
dialing instructions, for
modem, 130–132
dialing telephone numbers,
133
directories, 99–104
changing, 97, 99–100
changing default, 100
creating, 97, 100
deleting, 100–101
path in AUTOEXEC.BAT
file, 17
directory list, in File Manager, 91–92
disk space requirements, 1
Display Register in Calculator, 33
clearing, 35
Clipboard with, 35–36
tape entry in, 42–43
DOS prompt, 1
for starting Office PC
Shell, 5
temporary exit to, 10–11
dot, in Calendar, 69

E

editing function keys, in
Calendar, 67–68
EXP numerical display, 32

expanded memory, 12, 13
exponential functions,
52–53

F

fields, 105, 107, 119,
122–125
adding, 124
deleting, 124–125
name for, 110, 123
phone, 130
size of, 124
file format, for Calendar, 84
File Manager, 91–98
Clipboard with, 104
deleting files with, 94–95
directory management
with, 99–104
locating file name in, 92
Look feature in, 97
Mark feature in, 92
moving and renaming
files in, 95–96
Screen feature in,
101–104
starting, 91–92
transferring text from, 27
file names, locating in File
Manager, 92
files
creating for Notebook,
119–127
deleting in File Manager,
94–95

displaying list of, 99
printing Calendar to,
   85
retrieving for Notebook,
   106–107
saving Calculator tape
   as, 41
viewing contents of, 97
financial functions, with
   Calculator, 45–50
FIX numerical display, 32
floppy disks, 1
   installing Office PC on, 3
   running Office PC from, 9
   storage of, 3
foreground colors, 24
Format option, in Clipboard,
   30
Full Screen option, for file
   list display, 101–102
function keys
   in Calendar, 67–68
   for financial calculator,
      46–47
   for Scientific Calculator,
      51–54
future value, calculating, 47

G

GENERIC.PRD file, 88
Go to Date option, 77
Go to DOS command, 10
grand totals, from Calculator, 36–37
groups of files, working
   with, 93–94

H

Half Screen option, for file
   list display, 101
Hand-Fed Forms, for
   printer, 86
hard disks, installing Office
   PC on, 1–4
Hayes-compatible modem,
   129
header information, in File
   Manager, 91
Help feature
   for Calculator, 34
   for Calendar, 62–63, 68
   for Notebook, 106
   for Shell, 9
Hercules RamFont Card, 23
HEX numerical display, 32

I

insert mode, in Notebook,
   110
installation, 1n4
interest, calculating, 49–50

K

Key Function box, for calculator, 45, 55

L

labels, 107–110
   entering in records,
      121–122

LAN (local area network), 2
Line Draw, in Notebook,
119–121
List Display
adding record to, 110–111
creating, 125–127
deleting record from, 111
printing, 116–117
screen for, 105
sorting, 115–116
local area network (LAN), 2
logarithmic functions, 52–53
Look feature
for Calculator tape, 41–43
in File Manager, 97
Lotus/Intel/Microsoft (LIM)
expanded memory speci-
fications, 12

M

macro directory, 15
Macro Variable option, in
Clipboard, 30
mean, calculating, 57
Memo window, 61, 68–69
Memory Register in Calula-
tor, 36
tape entry in, 42–43
memory usage, tracing, 12
menu bar, for Calendar, 62
modem
dialing instructions for,
130–132

Notebook and, 129–133
setting up, 129–130
Move Days option, 78
moving text, with Clip-
board, 27–30

N

natural antilog, 53
natural log, 52
non-Shell-compatible
programs, moving text
between, 29–30
Notebook, 105–113. *See
also* List Display
creating file for,
119–127
editing record in,
107–110
exiting from, 113
file retrieval for,
106–107
Help for, 106
Line Draw in,
119–121
and modem, 129–133
screen colors for, 112
starting, 105–106
typeover or insert mode
for, 110
using Clipboard with, 27,
111–112
numerical display, in Calculator, 32

O

OCT numerical display, 32
Office PC Shell, 9–13
   adding program to menu,
     15–17
   customizing, 23–26
   deleting programs from,
     19–20
   starting, 5–8
   starting programs with, 9

P

parent directory, 99
password, 15, 84, 96
path command, 7, 17
phone field, 130
pi, 52
PlanPerfect, 27
population standard deviation, calculating, 57
population variance, calculating, 57
ports, 129
present value, calculating,
   47
printer, defining, for Calendar, 88–90
printing
   Calculator tape contents,
     40

with Calendar, 85–89
interrupting, 85
List Display, 116–117
records, 118
priorities, in To-Do List
   window, 83
profit margins, calculating,
   50
Program Information screen,
   16
programmer functions,
   in Calculator, 57–60
programs
   adding to Shell menu,
     15–17
   adding to slot occupied
     by other program,
     18–19
   deleting from Shell menu,
     19–20
   moving between,
     10–12
   moving in menu, 20–21
   starting with Shell menu,
     9
   startup letter for, 21
   switching directly
     between, 12

R

rebooting computer, 8
reciprocals, 52

records, 105
   editing in Notebook,
     107–110
   entering label in, 121–122
   printing, 118
registration number, 3
Repeat Performance pro-
   gram, 3

S

sample standard deviation,
   calculating, 57
sample variance, calculating, 57
Save option, in Clipboard,
   30
Scientific Calculator, 51–54
screen colors, 15, 23–25
   for Calculator, 37
   for Calendar, 84
   for Notebook, 112
Screen Copy feature, 28–30
Screen feature, for files and
   directories, 101–104
screen saver feature, 15
security of files, 96–97
Setup options, 23, 78–84
Shell. *See* Office PC Shell
Shell-compatible programs,
   moving text between,
   27–28

Shell key (Ctrl-F1), 10
Shell Memory Map, 12,
   13
shelling out, 10
sine, 53
sorting List Display,
   115–116
square of number, 52
square root, 52
squared entries, 57
standard deviation, calculating, 57
starting programs, with
   Shell menu, 9
startup letter, for programs,
   21
statistical functions, in
   Calculator, 55–57
storage of disks, 3
subtotals, 36

T

tangent, 54
tape. *See* Calculator tape
Tape key (F5), 39
telephone numbers, dialing,
   133
text, moving with Clip-
   board, 27–30
text editor, 6

time format, 15, 25–26, 79–80
To-Do List window, 61, 62, 73–75
  editing and deleting in, 75
  restoring deleted entry in, 75
  setting options for, 82–83
Tree directory structure, 102, 103–104
trigonometric functions, 53–54
typeover mode, in Note-book, 110

V

variance, calculating, 57

W

word search, through files, 97
WordPerfect
Text In/Out feature, 6
using Clipboard with, 27
work log, 15
write-protect notch, 4

Selections from The SYBEX Library

WORD PROCESSING

The ABC's of Microsoft Word (Third Edition)
Alan R. Neibauer
461pp. Ref. 604-9

This is for the novice WORD user who wants to begin producing documents in the shortest time possible. Each chapter has short, easy-to-follow lessons for both keyboard and mouse, including all the basic editing, formatting and printing functions. Version 5.0.

The ABC's of WordPerfect
Alan R. Neibauer
239pp. Ref. 425-9

This basic introduction to WordPefect consists of short, step-by-step lessons— for new users who want to get going fast. Topics range from simple editing and formatting, to merging, sorting, macros, and more. Includes version 4.2

The ABC's of WordPerfect 5
Alan R. Neibauer
283pp. Ref. 504-2

This introduction explains the basics of desktop publishing with WordPerfect 5: editing, layout, formatting, printing, sorting, merging, and more. Readers are shown how to use WordPerfect 5's new features to produce great-looking reports.

The ABC's of WordPerfect 5.1
Alan R. Neibauer
352pp. Ref. 672-3

Neibauer's delightful writing style makes this clear tutorial an especially effective learning tool. Learn all about 5.1's new drop-down menus and mouse capabilities that reduce the tedious memorization of function keys.

Advanced Techniques in Microsoft Word (Second Edition)
Alan R. Neibauer
462pp. Ref. 615-4

This highly acclaimed guide to WORD is an excellent tutorial for intermediate to advanced users. Topics include word processing fundamentals, desktop publishing with graphics, data management, and working in a multiuser environment. For Versions 4 and 5.

Advanced Techniques in MultiMate
Chris Gilbert
275pp. Ref. 412-7

A textbook on efficient use of MultiMate for business applications, in a series of self-contained lessons on such topics as multiple columns, high-speed merging, mailing-list printing and Key Procedures.

Advanced Techniques in WordPerfect 5
Kay Yarborough Nelson
586pp. Ref. 511-5

Now updated for Version 5, this invaluable guide to the advanced features of Word-Perfect provides step-by-step instructions and practical examples covering those specialized techniques which have most perplexed users—indexing, outlining, foreign-language typing, mathematical functions, and more.

The Complete Guide to MultiMate
Carol Holcomb Dreger
208pp. Ref. 229-9

This step-by-step tutorial is also an excellent reference guide to MultiMate features and uses. Topics include search/replace, library and merge functions, repagination, document defaults and more.

Encyclopedia WordPerfect 5.1
Greg Harvey
Kay Yarborough Nelson
1100pp. Ref. 676-6

This comprehensive, up-to-date Word-Perfect reference is a must for beginning and experienced users alike. With complete, easy-to-find information on every WordPerfect feature and command -- and it's organized by practical functions, with business users in mind.

Introduction to WordStar
Arthur Naiman
208pp. Ref. 134-9

This all time bestseller is an engaging first-time introduction to word processing as well as a complete guide to using WordStar—from basic editing to blocks, global searches, formatting, dot commands, SpellStar and MailMerge. Through Version 3.3.

Mastering DisplayWrite 4
Michael E. McCarthy

447pp. Ref. 510-7

Total training, reference and support for users at all levels—in plain, non-technical language. Novices will be up and running in an hour's time; everyone will gain complete word-processing and document-management skills.

Mastering Microsoft Word on the IBM PC (Fourth Edition)
Matthew Holtz

680pp. Ref. 597-2

This comprehensive, step-by-step guide details all the new desktop publishing developments in this versatile word processor, including details on editing, formatting, printing, and laser printing. Holtz uses sample business documents to demonstrate the use of different fonts, graphics, and complex documents. Includes Fast Track speed notes. For Versions 4 and 5.

Mastering MultiMate Advantage II
Charles Ackerman

407pp. Ref. 482-8

This comprehensive tutorial covers all the capabilities of MultiMate, and highlights the differences between MultiMate Advantage II and previous versions—in pathway support, sorting, math, DOS access, using dBASE III, and more. With many practical examples, and a chapter on the On-File database.

Mastering WordPerfect
Susan Baake Kelly

435pp. Ref. 332-5

Step-by-step training from startup to mastery, featuring practical uses (form letters, newsletters and more), plus advanced topics such as document security and macro creation, sorting and columnar math. Through Version 4.2.

Mastering WordPerfect 5
Susan Baake Kelly

709pp. Ref. 500-X

The revised and expanded version of this definitive guide is now on WordPerfect 5 and covers wordprocessing and basic desktop publishing. As more than 200,000 readers of the original edition can attest, no tutorial approaches it for clarity and depth of treatment. Sorting, line drawing, and laser printing included.

Mastering WordPerfect 5.1
Alan Simpson

1050pp. Ref. 670-7

The ultimate guide for the WordPerfect user. Alan Simpson, the "master communicator," puts you in charge of the latest features of 5.1: new dropdown menus and mouse capabilities, along with the desktop publishing, macro programming, and file conversion functions that have made WordPerfect the most popular word processing program on the market.

Mastering WordStar Release 5.5
Greg Harvey
David J. Clark

450pp. Ref. 491-7

This book is the ultimate reference book for the newest version of WordStar. Readers may use Mastering to look up any word processing function, including the new Version 5 and 5.5 features and enhancements, and find detailed instructions for fundamental to advanced operations.

Microsoft Word Instant Reference for the IBM PC
Matthew Holtz

266pp. Ref. 692-8

Turn here for fast, easy access to concise information on every command and feature of Microsoft Word version 5.0 -- for editing, formatting, merging, style sheets, macros, and more. With exact keystroke sequences, discussion of command options, and commonly-performed tasks.

Practical WordStar Uses
Julie Anne Arca

303pp. Ref. 107-1

A hands-on guide to WordStar and MailMerge applications, with solutions to comon problems and "recipes" for day-to-day tasks. Formatting, merge-printing and much more; plus a quick-reference command chart and notes on CP/M and PC-DOS. For Version 3.3.

Understanding Professional Write
Gerry Litton

400pp. Ref. 656-1

A complete guide to Professional Write that takes you from creating your first simple document, into a detailed description of all major aspects of the software. Special features place an emphasis on the use of different typestyles to create attractive documents as well as potential problems and suggestions on how to get around them.

Understanding WordStar 2000
David Kolodney
Thomas Blackadar
275pp. Ref. 554-9

This engaging, fast-paced series of tutorials covers everything from moving the cursor to print enhancements, format files, key glossaries, windows and MailMerge. With practical examples, and notes for former WordStar users.

Visual Guide to WordPerfect
Jeff Woodward
457pp. Ref. 591-3

This is a visual hands-on guide which is ideal for brand new users as the book shows each activity keystroke-by-keystroke. Clear illustrations of computer screen menus are included at every stage. Covers basic editing, formatting lines, paragraphs, and pages, using the block feature, footnotes, search and replace, and more. Through Version 5.

WordPerfect 5 Desktop Companion
SYBEX Ready Reference Series
Greg Harvey
Kay Yarborough Nelson
1006pp. Ref. 522-0

Desktop publishing features have been added to this compact encyclopedia. This title offers more detailed, cross-referenced entries on every software features including page formatting and layout, laser printing and word processing macros. New users of WordPerfect, and those new to Version 5 and desktop publishing will find this easy to use for on-the-job help.

WordPerfect Instant Reference
SYBEX Prompter Series
Greg Harvey
Kay Yarborough Nelson
254pp. Ref. 476-3, 4 ¾" × 8"

When you don't have time to go digging through the manuals, this fingertip guide offers clear, concise answers: command summaries, correct usage, and exact keystroke sequences for on-the-job tasks. Convenient organization reflects the structure of WordPerfect. Through Version 4.2.

WordPerfect 5 Instant Reference
SYBEX Prompter Series
Greg Harvey
Kay Yarborough Nelson
316pp. Ref. 535-2, 4 ¾" × 8"

This pocket-sized reference has all the program commands for the powerful WordPerfect 5 organized alphabetically for quick access. Each command entry has the exact key sequence, any reveal codes, a list of available options, and option-by-option discussions.

WordPerfect 5.1 Instant Reference
Greg Harvey
Kay Yarborough Nelson
252pp. Ref. 674-X

Instant access to all features and commands of WordPerfect 5.0 and 5.1, highlighting the newest software features. Complete, alphabetical entries provide exact key sequences, codes and options, and step-by-step instructions for many important tasks.

WordPerfect 5 Macro Handbook
Kay Yarborough Nelson
488pp. Ref. 483-6

Readers can create macros custom-tailored to their own needs with this excellent tutorial and reference. Nelson's expertise guides the WordPerfect 5 user through nested and chained macros, macro libraries, specialized macros, and much more.

WordPerfect 5.1 Tips and Tricks (Fourth Edition)
Alan R. Neibauer
675pp. Ref. 681-2

This new edition is a real timesaver. For on-the-job guidance and creative new uses, this title covers all versions of WordPerfect up to and including 5.1—streamlining documents, automating with macros, new print enhancements, and more.

WordStar Instant Reference
SYBEX Prompter Series
David J. Clark
314pp. Ref. 543-3, 4 ¾" × 8"

This quick reference provides reminders on the use of the editing, formatting, mailmerge, and document processing commands available through WordStar 4 and 5. Operations are organized alphabetically for easy access. The text includes a survey of the menu system and instructions for installing and customizing WordStar.

UTILITIES

Mastering the Norton Utilities
Peter Dyson
373pp. Ref. 575-1
In-depth descriptions of each Norton utility make this book invaluable for beginning and experienced users alike. Each utility is described clearly with examples and the text is organized so that readers can put Norton to work right away. Version 4.5.

Mastering PC Tools Deluxe
Peter Dyson
400pp. Ref. 654-5
A complete hands-on guide to the timesaving—and "lifesaving"—utility programs in Version 5.5 of PC Tools Deluxe. Contains concise tutorials and in-depth discussion of every aspect of using PC Tools—from high speed backups, to data recovery, to using Desktop applications.

Mastering SideKick Plus
Gene Weisskopf
394pp. Ref. 558-1
Employ all of Sidekick's powerful and expanded features with this hands-on guide to the popular utility. Features include comprehensive and detailed coverage of time management, note taking, outlining, auto dialing, DOS file management, math, and copy-and-paste functions.

Up & Running with Norton Utilities
Rainer Bartel
140pp. Ref. 659-6
Get up and running in the shortest possible time in just 20 lessons or "steps." Learn to restore disks and files, use UnErase, edit your floppy disks, retrieve lost data and more. Or use the book to evaluate the software before you purchase. Through Version 4.2.

Up & Running with PC Tools Deluxe 6
Thomas Holste
180pp. Ref.678-2
Learn to use this software program in just 20 basic steps. Readers get a quick, inexpensive introduction to using the Tools for disaster recovery, disk and file management, and more.

COMMUNICATIONS

Mastering Crosstalk XVI (Second Edition)
Peter W. Gofton
225pp. Ref. 642-1
Introducing the communications program Crosstalk XVI for the IBM PC. As well as providing extensive examples of command and script files for programming Crosstalk, this book includes a detailed description of how to use the program's more advanced features, such as windows, talking to mini or mainframe, customizing the keyboard and answering calls and background mode.

Mastering PROCOMM PLUS
Bob Campbell
400pp. Ref. 657-X
Learn all about communications and information retrieval as you master and use PROCOMM PLUS. Topics include choosing and using a modem; automatic dialing; using on-line services (featuring CompuServe) and more. Through Version 1.1b; also covers PROCOMM, the "shareware" version.

Mastering Serial Communications
Peter W. Gofton
289pp. Ref. 180-2
The software side of communications, with details on the IBM PC's serial programming, the XMODEM and Kermit protocols, non-ASCII data transfer, interrupt-level programming and more. Sample programs in C, assembly language and BASIC.

DESKTOP PUBLISHING

The ABC's of the New Print Shop
Vivian Dubrovin
340pp. Ref. 640-4
This beginner's guide stresses fun, practicality and original ideas. Hands-on tutorials show how to create greeting cards, invitations, signs, flyers, letterheads, banners, and calendars.

The ABC's of Ventura
Robert Cowart
Steve Cummings
390pp. Ref. 537-9

Created especially for new desktop publishers, this is an easy introduction to a complex program. Cowart provides details on using the mouse, the Ventura side bar, and page layout, with careful explanations of publishing terminology. The new Ventura menus are all carefully explained. For Version 2.

Mastering COREL DRAW!
Steve Rimmer
403pp. Ref. 685-5

This four-color tutorial and user's guide covers drawing and tracing, text and special effects, file interchange, and adding new fonts. With in-depth treatment of design principles. For version 1.1.

Mastering PageMaker on the IBM PC (Second Edition)
Antonia Stacy Jolles
384pp. Ref. 521-2

A guide to every aspect of desktop publishing with PageMaker: the vocabulary and basics of page design, layout, graphics and typography, plus instructions for creating finished typeset publications of all kinds.

Mastering Ventura (Second Edition)
Matthew Holtz
613pp. Ref. 581-6

A complete, step-by-step guide to IBM PC desktop publishing with Xerox Ventura Publisher. Practical examples show how to use style sheets, format pages, cut and paste, enhance layouts, import material from other programs, and more. For Version 2.

Understanding PFS: First Publisher
Gerry Litton
310pp. Ref. 616-2

This complete guide takes users from the basics all the way through the most complex features available. Discusses working with text and graphics, columns, clip art, and add-on software enhancements. Many page layout suggestions are introduced. Includes Fast Track speed notes.

Understanding PostScript Programming (Second Edition)
David A. Holzgang
472pp. Ref. 566-2

In-depth treatment of PostScript for programmers and advanced users working on custom desktop publishing tasks. Hands-on development of programs for font creation, integrating graphics, printer implementations and more.

Ventura Instant Reference SYBEX Prompter Series
Matthew Holtz
320pp. Ref. 544-1, 4 ¾" × 8"

This compact volume offers easy access to the complex details of Ventura modes and options, commands, side-bars, file management, output device configuration, and control. Written for versions through Ventura 2, it also includes standard procedures for project and job control.

Ventura Power Tools
Rick Altman
318pp. Ref. 592-1

Renowned Ventura expert, Rick Altman, presents strategies and techniques for the most efficient use of Ventura Publisher 2. This includes a power disk with DOS utilities which is specially designed for optimizing Ventura use. Learn how to soup up Ventura, edit CHP files, avoid design tragedies, handle very large documents, and improve form.

Your HP LaserJet Handbook
Alan R. Neibauer
564pp. Ref. 618-9

Get the most from your printer with this step-by-step instruction book for using LaserJet text and graphics features such as cartridge and soft fonts, type selection, memory and processor enhancements, PCL programming, and PostScript solutions. This hands-on guide provides specific instructions for working with a variety of software.

OPERATING SYSTEMS

The ABC's of DOS 4
Alan R. Miller
275pp. Ref. 583-2

This step-by-step introduction to using DOS 4 is written especially for beginners. Filled with simple examples, *The ABC's of DOS 4* covers the basics of hardware, software, disks, the system editor EDLIN, DOS commands, and more.

ABC's of MS-DOS
(Second Edition)
Alan R. Miller

233pp. Ref. 493-3

This handy guide to MS-DOS is all many PC users need to manage their computer files, organize floppy and hard disks, use EDLIN, and keep their computers organized. Additional information is given about utilities like Sidekick, and there is a DOS command and program summary. The second edition is fully updated for Version 3.3.

DOS Assembly Language Programming
Alan R. Miller

365pp. 487-9

This book covers PC-DOS through 3.3, and gives clear explanations of how to assemble, link, and debug 8086, 8088, 80286, and 80386 programs. The example assembly language routines are valuable for students and programmers alike.

DOS Instant Reference
SYBEX Prompter Series
Greg Harvey
Kay Yarborough Nelson

220pp. Ref. 477-1, 4 ¾" × 8"

A complete fingertip reference for fast, easy on-line help:command summaries, syntax, usage and error messages. Organized by function—system commands, file commands, disk management, directories, batch files, I/O, networking, programming, and more. Through Version 3.3.

DOS User's Desktop Companion
SYBEX Ready Reference Series
Judd Robbins

969pp. Ref. 505-0

This comprehensive reference covers DOS commands, batch files, memory enhancements, printing, communications and more information on optimizing each user's DOS environment. Written with step-by-step instructions and plenty of examples, this volume covers all versions through 3.3.

Encyclopedia DOS
Judd Robbins

1030pp. Ref. 699-5

A comprehensive reference and user's guide to all versions of DOS through 4.0. Offers complete information on every DOS command, with all possible switches and parameters -- plus examples of effective usage. An invaluable tool.

Essential OS/2
(Second Edition)
Judd Robbins

445pp. Ref. 609-X

Written by an OS/2 expert, this is the guide to the powerful new resources of the OS/2 operating system standard edition 1.1 with presentation manager. Robbins introduces the standard edition, and details multitasking under OS/2, and the range of commands for installing, starting up, configuring, and running applications. For Version 1.1 Standard Edition.

Essential PC-DOS
(Second Edition)
Myril Clement Shaw
Susan Soltis Shaw

332pp. Ref. 413-5

An authoritative guide to PC-DOS, including version 3.2. Designed to make experts out of beginners, it explores everything from disk management to batch file programming. Includes an 85-page command summary. Through Version 3.2.

Graphics Programming
Under Windows
Brian Myers
Chris Doner

646pp. Ref. 448-8

Straightforward discussion, abundant examples, and a concise reference guide to graphics commands make this book a must for Windows programmers. Topics range from how Windows works to programming for business, animation, CAD, and desktop publishing. For Version 2.

Hard Disk Instant Reference
SYBEX Prompter Series
Judd Robbins

256pp. Ref. 587-5, 4 ¾" × 8"

Compact yet comprehensive, this pocket-sized reference presents the essential information on DOS commands used in managing directories and files, and in optimizing disk configuration. Includes a survey of third-party utility capabilities. Through DOS 4.0.

The IBM PC-DOS Handbook
(Third Edition)
Richard Allen King

359pp. Ref. 512-3

A guide to the inner workings of PC-DOS 3.2, for intermediate to advanced users and programmers of the IBM PC series. Topics include disk, screen and port control, batch files, networks, compatibility, and more. Through Version 3.3.

SYBEX Computer Books
are different.

Here is why . . .

At SYBEX, each book is designed with you in mind. Every manuscript is carefully selected and supervised by our editors, who are themselves computer experts. We publish the best authors, whose technical expertise is matched by an ability to write clearly and to communicate effectively. Programs are thoroughly tested for accuracy by our technical staff. Our computerized production department goes to great lengths to make sure that each book is well-designed.

In the pursuit of timeliness, SYBEX has achieved many publishing firsts. SYBEX was among the first to integrate personal computers used by authors and staff into the publishing process. SYBEX was the first to publish books on the CP/M operating system, microprocessor interfacing techniques, word processing, and many more topics.

Expertise in computers and dedication to the highest quality product have made SYBEX a world leader in computer book publishing. Translated into fourteen languages, SYBEX books have helped millions of people around the world to get the most from their computers We hope we have helped you, too.

For a complete catalog of our publications:

SYBEX, Inc. 2021 Challenger Drive, #100, Alameda, CA 94501
Tel: (415) 523-8233/(800) 227-2346 Telex: 336311
Fax: (415) 523-2373